Victorian
DREAM HOMES

 Home Planners, Inc.

Designed and Produced by Home Planners, Inc.
Book Designer: Kathleen A. Koopman

Published by Home Planners, Inc.
Editorial and Corporate Offices:
3275 West Ina Road, Suite 110
Tucson, Arizona 85741

Distribution Center:
29323 Lorie Lane
Wixom, Michigan 48393

Charles W. Talcott, Chairman
Rickard Bailey, President and Publisher
Cindy J. Coatsworth, Publications Manager
Paulette Mulvin, Editor

Photo Credits
Front Cover: Greg Ryan/Sally Beyer
Back Cover: Andrew D. Lautman

10 9 8 7 6 5 4 3 2

Library of Congress Catalog Card Number: 91-072540
ISBN: 0-918894-90-5 paperback
ISBN: 0-918894-91-3 hardback

On the front cover: Our charming Queen Anne front cover design is plan M3382.
For more information about this home, see page 74.
On the back cover: This inviting Queen Anne design is our plan M9055.
For more information about this home, see page 18.

TABLE OF CONTENTS

EDITOR'S NOTE

Within these pages are the finest Victorian and Victorian-inspired Farmhouse designs available on the market today. Three master architectural design firms—Larry W. Garnett & Associates, Inc.; Home Planners, Inc.; and Historical Replications, Inc.—are each showcased in separate sections featuring first the designer's special portfolio of Victorian homes followed by a delightful collection of Farmhouse plans. Experts in traditional home design, these designers interpret both cherished styles in distinctive ways, maintaining historical integrity while adding modern livability. And because complete blueprint packages are available for every spectacular home presented, the Victorian and Farmhouse plans you see here can be extended beyond mere admiration to actual construction and day-to-day enjoyment. If you've been searching for a home that is a reflection of this era of architecture, this book is the answer to your quest.

THE VICTORIAN ROMANCE

ew periods of architecture have received as much attention and spawned as many devotees as the 70 years from 1840 to 1910 known as the Victorian Era. Named after Queen Victoria, who enjoyed an uncommonly long reign (1837–1901), this period captures the imagination of so many people because so much seemed to change and blossom over its duration. Even though the architecture of the time had its antecedents in the Gothic Revival that began a few years earlier, it is the Victorian Era that most people embrace because it epitomizes what had been lacking or stale in architecture for hundreds of years: liveliness, whimsy and, above all, freedom of expression.

Like most movements that develop and evolve over a broad expanse of time, no single individual or event seemed to drive the Victorian Revolution. Rather, a series of stirrings, ideas and concepts— aided by technology—pushed the movement from one stage to another until it reached a grand climax near the end of the century.

REACTION TO CLASSICISM
First came a general uneasiness and backlash against the classicism of the early 19th Century. Greek Revival, characterized by formality, symmetry and "high-style," was perfectly suited to a new Republic that was enjoying the fruits of democracy and its newly won independence. However, after some 40 years of architecture marked by equal-spaced columns, carved entablature and severe granite facades, some people began to look for a fresh pattern for public and private residences. Andrew Jackson Downing supplied this when he published his *Victorian Cottage Residences* in 1842. The first popular pattern book for house styles, this publication supplied an alternative to the "perfect" Greek house facade—new fashions that took their cue from Medieval precedents and the Italian Renaissance.

Still anchored to antiquity and thus acceptable, this new style began to soften the edges of buildings, offering curved lines, arched windows, fretwork and even spires. Soon neighborhoods began to sport an "Italianate" cottage or "Medieval" manse worked in between imposing Greek residences. Suddenly, people had a choice and it was permissible to experiment with and broaden architectural expression, even going so far as to include exotic Egyptian or Oriental-inspired dwellings. Like a breath of fresh air, the winds of the Gothic Revival swept throughout England and America and the new architectural freedom was soon in full swing.

Classic Greek Revival

Medieval Architecture

HELP FROM TECHNOLOGY

Intellectual and artistic fervor alone would not have carried the movement far had not industrialization and technology been there to bear it up. The Industrial Revolution in both England and the United States supplied the material that fueled the fire of the New Freedom. The new wealth created by industrialization meant that an emerging middle and upper-middle class now had the resources to begin building homes of greater distinction and individualization. The "railroading" of America brought lumber, glass and metals in plentiful supply, while newly forged cutting and carving tools meant that craftsmen could give full vent to their woodworking acumen. Later in the century, the new "balloon-framing" technique freed builders from heavy, restrictive timber-framing methods and allowed houses to be built faster, more economically and, important to the movement, with many more asymmetrical wings, appendages and juttings.

No surprise that as Gothic Revival turned to full Victorian Romanticism, houses began to exhibit more and more handiwork in all areas. Builders during the High Victorian Era sought to outdo one another with more spindles, scallops, fretwork, brackets and carvings than the house before. Buildings sprouted domes and spires. Gables protruded in every direction. Floors overhung floors and were propped up by elaborately decorated columns. Perhaps the zenith of the movement came with the construction of the Carson Mansion in Eureka, California in 1886. Trying to please a local lumber baron, builders outdid themselves with a 5-story Queen Anne "castle" that sported multiple Gothic towers, exquisitely carved gables and friezes, finials on every conceivable roof cap, and a magnificent wraparound porch decorated with heavy balls and rings.

DEFINING THE PERIOD

Although it is romantically engaging to view the Victorian Era as an out-of-control architectural whirlwind sweeping toward the end of the century, the fact is that it was more prosaic than that. A number of architectural influences flourished at the time, but they were mostly derivative, and it is helpful in understanding the styles of the era to look at the various elements and how they interacted. For this discussion, I am indebted to Virginia and Lee McAlester, whose book, *A Field Guide to American Houses* (Alfred A. Knopf, 1984), does the best and quickest job of sorting out these styles and establishing their chronology.

Gothic Revival Architecture

ROMANTIC BEGINNINGS

As already noted, *Gothic Revival* (1840-1880) was a direct reaction to—or relief from—the strict rules of form and composition established by Early Classical Revival and particularly Greek Revival. Gothic Revival style made use of a steeply pitched roof with cross-gables and windows patterned in a distinctive Gothic or Medieval shape. Probably the most characteristic feature of this style is the decorative *vergeboard*, or gable trim piece, that was often cut in scallop, fleur-de-lis or other patterns with the newly perfected scroll saw. More popular for rural areas, the design was too oversized and excessive for smaller urban lots. Thus, while heralding a new departure from classical symmetry and restraint, the style never really caught on widely and was on the wane by 1880. Nevertheless, it did set the precedent for future experimentation and its "dare-to-

The Carson Mansion

Italianate Style

Second Empire Style

be-different" attitude got the Romantic Era underway.

Italianate Style (1840-1885), which surfaced about the same time as Gothic Revival, began in England as part of the Picaresque movement and was even more opposed to formal classical ideals. It emphasized Italian villa-style architecture with low-pitched roofs, wide overhangs, and tall, narrow windows frequently elaborated with hooded crowns or "eyebrows." A common characteristic was a central tower or cupola rising above the other parts of the building, often sporting a curved mansard roof. Popularized by Andrew Jackson Downing in his pattern books, this style was admired by many richer clientele and was widely built in various forms until the financial panic of 1873 and the resulting economic collapse. Built mostly of masonry, these houses contributed more to the romantic freedom of the era than they did to the craftsmanship and techniques employed in later wood-sided Victorian houses.

MIDDLE VICTORIAN PERIOD

Second Empire Style (1855-1885) took a few cues from the Italianate houses that were in vogue a few years earlier, but added modern rooflines and cornices taken from the French fashions of the day. Named after the reign of Napoleon III (1852-1870), France's Second Empire exerted a tremendous influence on the architecture of the period by sponsoring exhibitions in Paris in 1855 and 1867. The most striking characteristic of this style is the dual-pitched, hipped mansard roof, named after 17th-Century French architect Francois Mansart whose work was revived at the time. These roof lines—commonly straight, straight with a flair, or slightly concave—graced all sides of the building,

as well as any cupolas or towers that ascended above the main structure. Dormer windows appeared in abundance on Second Empire homes, and many featured Italianate brackets at the cornices and decorative iron railings or crests at the highest roof line. Many public buildings or private residences were built or remodeled in this style in the mid-1800s, but like the Italianate, this European-influenced style disappeared quickly following the financial panic of 1873 and the economic hard times that followed.

Stick Style (1860-1890) refocused builders on the use of wood instead of masonry as was often used in European styles. However, unlike their romantic Gothic forebears which made use of fancy

Stick Style

fretwork and detailing at doors, windows and cornices, Stick houses used the plane of the wall as a decorative element. Structures were quite simple and box-like, but the faces of walls were "tricked up" with patterns of horizontal, vertical or diagonal boards raised from the wall surface for emphasis. In addition, exposed and embellished trusses were shown under the peaks

Queen Anne Style

of gables and beneath overhanging eaves. Called "stickwork," this construction technique carried the romantic notion of "honesty of style" since it showed the structural nature of the building. However, unlike earlier half-timbering which was integral to the framing of the building, stickwork was simply applied over light balloon framing and had nothing to do with supporting the structure. Nonetheless, proponents argued the value of the look with its return to natural materials and the style was very popular well into the 1880s in areas with an abundance of lumber.

HIGH VICTORIAN PERIOD

Queen Anne Style (1880-1910) was the culmination of the romantic quest for fine craftsmanship, abundance of detail and free individual expression. Popularized by a group of 19th-Century architects led by Richard Norman Shaw, the name was actually misapplied and inappropriate, since Queen Anne's reign (1702-1714) produced more formal and heavy Renaissance-Style architecture. Nevertheless, the romantic notion of this Medieval period was more important than actuality, and the name quickly caught on and stuck. At first characterized by heavier half-timbering in England, the Queen Anne Style rapidly evolved in this country to more elaborate and delicate structures featuring patterned shingles, carved fretwork, finials and lacelike wooden ornamentation throughout the building.

Two of the most common sub-types of the Queen Anne Style are defined by their particular type of decorative detailing. *Spindlework* types feature delicately turned porch supports and spindle-type ornamentation, particularly in porch balustrades or as a frieze hung from the porch ceiling. Often referred to as "gingerbread," spindlework ornamentation is commonly found in gable ends and under wall overhangs. *Free Classic* types use classical columns, rather than turned posts, as porch supports. These porch-support columns are often grouped together in units of two or three. Other characteristics are formal dentils at the cornice line, Palladian windows and small front gables or pediments.

Queen Anne Victorians dominated residential building from about 1880 until 1900 and persisted in many parts of the United States through the first decade of this century. The style disappeared most quickly from the Northeast and Eastern Seaboard, where it was replaced principally by Colonial Revival fervor. However, excellent examples of Queen Anne Style continued to be built after this time in the San Francisco area, the Northwest and parts of the South.

Spindlework

Free Classic Columns

Folk Victorian

TURN-OF-THE-CENTURY ADAPTATIONS

The Romantic Movement was so pervasive that even as a new century dawned with divergent architectural prospects, Victorian influences still lingered and evolved in the twilight of its glory.

A fanciful new *Shingle Style* (1890-1910) enjoyed brief popularity at the turn of the century, especially in seaside resorts of the Northeastern United States. Rather than making use of fancy woodwork or detailing at doors, windows, cornices and other areas, the Shingle Style used a "cocoon" of shingles to envelop a complex architectural style. In fact, this skin of shingles often hid a number of interesting and dichotomous variations in forms and styles. However, still derivative, the Shingle Style borrowed the wide porches, asymmetrical forms and patterned shingles from the Queen Anne Style and the gambrel roofs and lean-to additions from the newly emerging Colonial Revival Style.

A by-product of the Victorian Era—lacelike porch detail and fancy brackets under the eaves—found its way into the simplest housing forms. After 1870, many basic folk houses began to sport Queen-Anne-Style porch supports, saw-cut cornice brackets and spindlework friezes suspended from porch ceilings. Although much less elaborate than their Victorian sisters, these houses became prevalent enough that a new style, *Folk Victorian* (1870–1910), was born. Local carpenters made good use of pre-cut Victorian trim pieces available at lumber yards and soon many people were enjoying front porches and gabled facades with a quaint Victorian look. After about 1910, these Folk Victorians—or Symmetrical Victorians as they are called by some scholars—generally lost favor as the country finally got its fill of fancy Victorian detailing and turned to other house styles for the new century.

GONE BUT NOT FORGOTTEN

The Victorian Era had a long, full flower of nearly 70 years. The emotional appeal of this family of fanciful, delicate, decorative architectural styles was so strong that it took the harsh realities of a World War and the nihilism of the 1920s to dispel it. Yet, the romance of this era never really died. Whenever society has too much of modern technology, warfare or rampant commercialism, it inevitably recycles itself back to an era that is quieter, softer and more romantic.

Grand Victorian Style is, after all, one of those rare pleasures that must be experienced more with the heart than with the intellect—to be viewed and appreciated without regard to cost, reason or rationale. Victorians exist simply to be admired and loved—one of the last, great romantic adventures in Architecture!

Rickard Bailey
Home Planners, Inc.

Shingle Style

LARRY W. GARNETT & ASSOCIATES, INC.

Larry W. Garnett & Associates, Inc. of Pasadena, Texas began designing homes for Houston-area residents in 1977. For the past ten years, Garnett & Associates has been marketing designs nationally to both individuals and builders, and the company's houses have now been built throughout the United States, and in Canada, Australia and Ireland.

A member of the American Institute of Building Design, Garnett & Associates has received numerous awards from the Texas Institute of Building Design, including several first-place awards for planned developments and builders' model homes. The firm recently received an award from the American Institute of Building Design for a custom home in Nashville.

In March 1985, the "Wall Street Journal Report," a syndicated television program, featured Garnett & Associates on a segment involving the increasing popularity of new Victorian homes and the availability of stock plans and designs for such homes. Recently, the company had the opportunity to design a twelve-home historic Hawaiian development in Kailua, Hawaii. This award-winning project features architecture that was popular in Hawaii in the early 1900s.

The company's plans have been published in such magazines as *House Beautiful, Country Living, Home,* and *Professional Builder.* Garnett's Victorian-inspired designs are featured each month in a regular column in *Victoria* magazine.

"American residential design during the last half of the 19th Century was dominated by the Victorian Style of architecture," relates Garnett. "Today, the homes from this period are considered by many to be symbols of the creative freedom and optimism that was prevalent during this period of rapid industrialization. While mass-produced tools and building materials were inexpensive and readily available, the homes were still constructed by artisans who took great pride in showcasing their craftsmanship. Furthermore, the designs for these homes were inspired by the classical architectural elements and forms that have withstood the test of time. Various details, such as gables, chimneys, steep rooflines and porches, provided traditional forms that were easily understood and emotionally comforting. The homes in this section utilize these same traditional values and provide a sense of continuity by linking the present to the past.

"Our Victorian and Farmhouse plans were designed to recapture the harmony of style and timeless design of this bygone era. Along with this nostalgic charm, we wanted to create homes that would become retreats from today's fast-paced society, with spacious living areas, multi-purpose media centers, and elegant master suites. The design knowledge we have accumulated from open-concept space planning, along with the realization that people also desire private, personal areas, has resulted in a blend of expansive areas with unobstructed views, along with versatile alcoves and cozy nooks for privacy.

"Based on original designs of the late 19th and early 20th Centuries, these homes range from the elaborate and ornate Queen Anne Style to the simple, decoratively detailed Folk Victorian Style. In addition, there are several examples of the Shingle Style, which were inspired by the fashionable summer resorts of the East Coast, with their massive, irregular rooflines, numerous windows and uniform shingle siding.

"As you browse through the following pages, we hope you agree that these designs offer a lasting tribute to the design integrity of the Victorian Era. Perhaps one of them will not only recall for you the comfort and serenity of the past, but also fulfill all the requirements you may have for your ideal home."

Classic exterior detailing transforms this otherwise simple design into an elegant Victorian cottage. The wraparound veranda is a perfect place for outdoor living. Inside, a raised foyer overlooks the large formal dining area and the living room. The kitchen offers a large built-in pantry, a bay-windowed breakfast nook and an island cooktop. Bedroom 2 features a fourteen-foot ceiling with bookcases, and a plant ledge above the windows. Bedroom 3 has a delightful windowed alcove perfect for a reading or study area. A French door opens from the master bedroom to the veranda. The master bath features a corner tub and glass-enclosed shower, along with a dressing table and plenty of linen storage.

9' Clg. Throughout
Unless Otherwise Noted

WIDTH 52'
DEPTH 63'

DESIGN M9049
BEDROOMS 3
BATHROOMS 2
SQUARE FOOTAGE 1,891
PRICE A4

REAR VIEW

Porch

French Doors

Util.

French Door

2-Car Garage

Master Bedroom
15' x 14'-4"

Linen

Bath

Dining
11'-4" x 12'

Kitchen
12' x 12'-4"

Cathedral Clg.

Desk

Bedroom 3
11'-4" x 10'

Living Room
18' x 14'

Foyer

Bedroom 2
11'-4" x 14'

Veranda

WIDTH 56' 4"
DEPTH 81' 10"

9' Clg. Throughout
Unless Otherwise Noted

The ornate turned posts at the veranda, along with delicate wood molding and carved gable brackets, give this Queen Anne Style cottage lasting elegance. The dining area features triple French doors and a cathedral ceiling. Bedroom 3 offers a built-in desk, making it a perfect optional study. The master suite has French doors opening to a covered porch and a large bath with a walk-in closet, plenty of linen storage, and a glass-enclosed shower. The steep-pitched roof offers the opportunity to utilize the attic space for a 14' x 19' bonus room with a ½ bath. Plans are included for this option, showing a circular staircase located at the foyer closet area. An attached two-car garage is located conveniently just off the handy utility room.

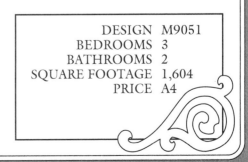

DESIGN M9051
BEDROOMS 3
BATHROOMS 2
SQUARE FOOTAGE 1,604
PRICE A4

The prominent octagon-shaped turret with leaded-glass transom windows is a Queen Anne Style detail typical of only the most elaborate one-story designs from the turn of the century. Inside, it creates a delightful space that can function as a conversation alcove or a study area. The kitchen has a center island and plenty of cabinet space. A ten-foot ceiling and three full-length windows in the dining room give this area a spacious feeling. The side porch can be connected with a covered walk to the two-car detached garage, for which plans are included. The master bedroom has a ten-foot ceiling and a bay-windowed sitting area. Bedrooms 2 and 3 both have walk-in closets, while bedroom 3 offers a corner window seat.

8' Clg. Throughout
Unless Otherwise Noted

WIDTH 45' 6"
DEPTH 47'

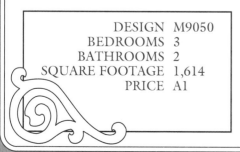

DESIGN	M9050
BEDROOMS	3
BATHROOMS	2
SQUARE FOOTAGE	1,614
PRICE	A1

QUEEN ANNE COTTAGE

Breakfast 10' x 10'

Util.

Porch

French Doors

Kitchen 10' x 12'

French Doors

Living Room 16' x 18' 10' Clg.

Master Bedroom 13'-4" x 16'-4"

Dining 13' x 10'-8" 10' Clg.

Hutch

Foyer

Bath Cath. Clg.

Bath 2

Niche

Linen

Bedroom 3 11'-4" x 13'

Bedroom 2 11'-4" x 12' 10' Clg.

Veranda

WIDTH 48' 4"
DEPTH 64' 8"

9' Clg. Throughout
Unless Otherwise Noted

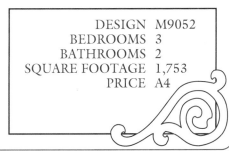

REAR VIEW

The fine wood trim and copper roof at the box-bay window, along with the ornate fretwork and turned posts at the veranda, add a certain degree of elegance to this Queen Anne Style cottage. A leaded-glass front door opens to a foyer with built-in display niches on each side. The formal dining area has a ten-foot ceiling and built-in hutch. Four full-length windows offer an unobstructed view from the living area to the covered porch and rear yard. The kitchen overlooks a breakfast area with six large windows and a pair of French doors. The master bedroom also has French doors opening to the large rear porch. The master bath has a dramatic cathedral ceiling and a garden tub with angled glass windows above.

DESIGN M9052
BEDROOMS 3
BATHROOMS 2
SQUARE FOOTAGE 1,753
PRICE A4

While much less elaborate than some other Victorian designs, the intersecting roof lines, arch-top windows with shutters, and detailed corner pilasters give this home a casual, yet distinctive appearance. An eight-foot-wide veranda provides plenty of room for outdoor entertaining. Inside, the large foyer opens to the formal dining area. A thirteen-foot raised ceiling with blocked panel trim and crown molding adds interest to the living room. French doors lead to a private library with built-in bookcases and a window seat. The secluded master suite offers a walk-in closet and an elegant bath with garden tub and glass-enclosed shower. Two large bedrooms each have walk-in closets and ceilings that slope from six feet to nine feet in height. Plans for a detached garage are included.

FIRST FLOOR

SECOND FLOOR

9' Clg. Throughout
First and Second Floor
Unless Otherwise Noted

WIDTH 54'
DEPTH 53' 8"

DESIGN	M9008
BEDROOMS	3
BATHROOMS	2½
FIRST FLOOR	1,653 Sq. Ft.
SECOND FLOOR	613 Sq. Ft.
TOTAL	2,266 Sq. Ft.
PRICE	A4

GARAGE

2-Car Garage

French Doors

Master Bedroom
13'-4" x 17'
11' Clg.

Bath

Breakfast
8' x 8'

Kitchen
16' x 12'

Bath 2

French Door

Util.

Bedroom 3
12' x 12'
11' Step-Up Clg.

Dining
15'-8" x 10'-8"
12' Clg.

Raised
Foyer

Bedroom 2
13' x 11'-4"

French
Doors

Living Room
21' x 14'-4"
12' Clg.

Veranda

FIRST FLOOR

Bath 3

Plant Shelves

Foyer Below

Gameroom
18'-8" x 15'-4"

SECOND FLOOR

9' Clg. Throughout
Unless Otherwise Noted

REAR VIEW

WIDTH 50' 4"
DEPTH 58'

A seven-foot-wide veranda with ornate fretwork, porch railing and intricate post brackets, along with a copper-topped box window, provide this home with old-fashioned charm and romance. Inside, the raised foyer opens into the living and dining areas. Stairs lead to the second-floor game room and bath. Bedrooms 2 and 3 each have French doors that open to the front veranda. The secluded master bedroom has French doors, while the spacious master bath features a garden tub with adjacent glass-enclosed shower, along with a large walk-in closet. The kitchen has ample cabinet space, a center work island, and a magnificent view through the breakfast area to the rear yard. Plans for a detached two-car garage are included with this design.

DESIGN	M9030
BEDROOMS	3
BATHROOMS	3
FIRST FLOOR	1,837 Sq. Ft.
SECOND FLOOR	445 Sq. Ft.
TOTAL	2,282 Sq. Ft.
PRICE	A4

Elaborate spindlework and ornate porch posts, along with detailed block-paneled trim at the symmetrical gables, give this Queen Anne Style two-story charm and elegance. The living room has a fireplace as its focal point, while at the same time providing a view of the built-in media center. The large kitchen opens to the dining area, and also has access to the garage and laundry room. The master bedroom is truly a luxurious private retreat. The sitting area has a built-in media center for audio and video equipment. The master bath contains a glass-enclosed shower and His and Hers lavatories. Two additional bedrooms, each with a walk-in closet, share a hall bath.

Books

Bath 2

Bedroom 2
12'-8" x 11'-4"

Bedroom 3
10' x 11'-8"

Media Center

Sitting Area
9'-8" x 10'

Balcony

Bath

Master Bedroom
15' x 18'-8"

SECOND FLOOR

WIDTH 45'
DEPTH 53'

2-Car Garage

Porch

French Door

Util.

Kitchen
10' x 12'

Stor.

Dining
10' x 10'

1/2 Bath

Media Center

Foyer

Living Room
15' x 18'-8"

Veranda

9' Clg. Throughout First and Second Floors

FIRST FLOOR

DESIGN	M9053
BEDROOMS	3
BATHROOMS	2½
FIRST FLOOR	811 Sq. Ft.
SECOND FLOOR	1,067 Sq. Ft.
TOTAL	1,878 Sq. Ft.
PRICE	A4

REAR VIEW

Dining
16' x 10'

Porch
French Door

Kitchen
11' x 10'

Util.

36" High Wall

FIRST FLOOR

Living Room
16' x 22'

Foyer

Veranda

9' Clg. Throughout First Floor

Bedrom 2
10' x 11'

Bath 2

Bedrom 3
10' x 12'

Bath
Cath. Clg.

Linen

Foyer Below

Master Bedroom
12' x 19'

SECOND FLOOR

8' Clg. Throughout Second Floor

A steep-pitched roof, decorative shingles at the front gable, and a wraparound veranda accent this relatively economical Queen Anne Style design. Inside, an impressive foyer opens to the second-floor balcony. The living area is separated from the dining room with a half wall and paneled columns. An efficiently designed kitchen serves the dining room. The laundry room opens to the rear porch, which can be connected with a covered walk to the detached two-car garage, for which plans are included. Upstairs, leaded-glass windows fill the balcony and upper foyer with natural light. The master bedroom offers a walk-in closet, in addition to a mirrored closet in the bath area.

DESIGN	M9054
BEDROOMS	3
BATHROOMS	2½
FIRST FLOOR	860 Sq. Ft.
SECOND FLOOR	818 Sq. Ft.
TOTAL	1,678 Sq. Ft.
PRICE	A1

WIDTH 37'
DEPTH 33' 10"

QUEEN ANNE

With its exceptional detail and proportions, this home is reminiscent of the Queen Anne Style. Turned posts resting on brick pedestals support a raised-gable entry to the veranda. The foyer opens to a living area with a bay-windowed alcove and a fireplace with flanking bookshelves. A large walk-in pantry and box window at the sink are special features in the kitchen. Natural light fills the breakfast area with a full-length bay window and a French door. Upstairs, the master bedroom offers unsurpassed elegance and convenience. The sitting area has an eleven-foot ceiling with arch-top windows. The bath area features a large walk-in closet, His and Hers lavatories, and plenty of linen storage. Plans for a two-car detached garage are included.

FIRST FLOOR

8' Clg. Throughout

SECOND FLOOR

WIDTH 39' 8"
DEPTH 39' 2"

DESIGN M9055
BEDROOMS 3
BATHROOMS 2½
FIRST FLOOR 997 Sq. Ft.
SECOND FLOOR 1,069 Sq. Ft.
TOTAL 2,066 Sq. Ft.
PRICE A5

FIRST FLOOR

2-Car Garage

Porch

French Door

Breakfast
10' x 10'

Util.

Storage

Pantry

Media Center

Kitchen
16' x 10'

Family Room
18'-4" x 14'-8"

Desk Below
Landing

Seating

Dining
11'-4" x 13'

Study
12'-8" x 10'

Foyer

French Door

Porch

Living Room
14'-8" x 12'-8"

Arbor

First Floor

10' Clg. Throughout First Floor

SECOND FLOOR

Bedroom 4
12' x 11'

Bath 3

Bedroom 3
13' x 11'

32" High
Cabinet

Linen

Seat

Bath 2

Bath

Linen

Bedroom 2
12' x 13'

Master Bedroom
20'-4" x 14'-4"

Alcove
10' x 7'

9' Clg. Throughout Second Floor

WIDTH 46' 6"
DEPTH 65' 8"

Inside this charming turn-of-the-century design, classical columns separate the foyer and dining room. A French door opens from the living room to a lattice-covered side arbor. Double doors in both the living and family rooms provide access to a bay-windowed study with built-in book-cases and a desk. The large family room contains a fireplace, media cabinet, and a serving bar open from the kitchen. A six-foot curved picture window offers a full view of the rear porch from the breakfast and kitchen areas. Upstairs, the master suite features an elegant bath with a garden tub inset in a bay window, and a walk-in closet. Bedrooms 3 and 4 share a bath, while bedroom 2 has a private bath and a bay-windowed alcove.

DESIGN	M9056
BEDROOMS	4
BATHROOMS	3½
FIRST FLOOR	1,354 Sq. Ft.
SECOND FLOOR	1,418 Sq. Ft.
TOTAL	2,772 Sq. Ft.
PRICE	A4

REAR VIEW

Classical columns on brick pedestals support a seven-foot veranda, beyond which extends an 11' x 18' lattice-covered arbor. In addition to a thirteen-foot vaulted ceiling, the dining room has French doors that open to both the rear yard and the front veranda. The living room has a bay window and two flanking windows. A breakfast alcove with expansive windows is part of the efficient kitchen. French doors and a bay window provide a comfortable retreat in the secluded master suite. Upstairs, the balcony overlooks a dramatic staircase and foyer below. Three additional bedrooms each have walk-in closets and special window treatments. The door of the attached two-car garage can be located at either side or to the rear.

DESIGN	M9009
BEDROOMS	4
BATHROOMS	2½
FIRST FLOOR	1,351 Sq. Ft.
SECOND FLOOR	862 Sq. Ft.
TOTAL	2,213 Sq. Ft.
PRICE	A4

FIRST FLOOR

2-Car Garage

Util.

Linen Bath

Breakfast
8' x 8'

Hamper

Master Bedroom
13'-8" x 13'-4"

Kitchen

French Door

French Door

Dining
10' x 12'-8"
13' Clg.

Gallery

Foyer

French Door

Living Room
15'-4" x 16'

Piazza

Veranda

9' Clg. Throughout
Unless Otherwise Noted

REAR VIEW

Bedroom 4
12'-4" x 13'-4"

Bedroom 3
13'-8" x 13'-4"
11' Clg.

Laundry
Chute

Bath 2

42" High Wall

Bedroom 2
15'-4" x 11'-4"
Cathedral Clg.

SECOND FLOOR

WIDTH   46' 8"
WIDTH WITH PIAZZA   58' 4"
DEPTH   72' 4"

Queen Anne Victorians were the dominant style of homes during the last part of the 19th Century. Although the exterior of this home is more restrained than many of the typical Queen Anne examples, still present are the decorative front-facing gable, porch fretwork, and steeply pitched roof lines. Leaded-glass windows admit light into the spacious foyer, which is separated from the formal dining room by paneled columns. The private master suite includes a bay-windowed sitting room and spectacular bath. The kitchen overlooks a breakfast area with double French doors that open to a large rear porch. Upstairs, three bedrooms and a game room provide plenty of living space for a large family. Plans for a detached two-car garage are included.

DESIGN M9057
BEDROOMS 4
BATHROOMS 2½
FIRST FLOOR 1,686 Sq. Ft.
SECOND FLOOR 965 Sq. Ft.
TOTAL 2,651 Sq. Ft.
PRICE A5

FIRST FLOOR

9' Clg. Throughout First Floor

SECOND FLOOR

8' Clg. Throughout Second Floor

WIDTH 43' 10"
DEPTH 54' 8"

9' Clg. Throughout First Floor

Bath 3

Porch

Breakfast
11' x 11'

French Door

Util.

Family Room
12' x 15'-4"
10' Clg.

Living Room
17' x 15'-4"

Kitchen
14' x 12'

2-Way Fireplace

Media Center

French Door

Veranda

Dining
12'-4" x 12'-4"

FIRST FLOOR

Bath

Bedroom 3
12'-4" x 10'-4"

Master Bedroom
17'-4" x 11'-4"

Bath 2

Sitting Area
12' Clg.

Window Seat

Bedroom 2
12'-4" x 14'

8' Clg. Throughout Second Floor
Unless Otherwise Noted

SECOND FLOOR

WIDTH 52' 8"
DEPTH 33' 4"

Certainly, the most dominant feature of the Queen Anne Style is the tower at the front of the house. This design offers not only an octagon-shaped tower, but also ornate bay windows and decorative gable shingles. Inside, a two-way fireplace is functional in both the living room and family area. Highlights of the kitchen include a walk-in pantry, center work island, and box window at the sink. A French door opens from the breakfast room to a rear porch. The utility room leads to a detached two-car garage, for which the plans are included. Upstairs, the master bedroom is accented with a sitting area defined by a twelve-foot octagon-shaped ceiling. Two additional bedrooms share a dressing area and bath.

DESIGN	M9058
BEDROOMS	3
BATHROOMS	3
FIRST FLOOR	1,348 Sq. Ft.
SECOND FLOOR	1,058 Sq. Ft.
TOTAL	2,406 Sq. Ft.
PRICE	A4

With a veranda wrapping around an octagon-shaped turret, decorative shingle siding, and double posts placed on brick pedestals, this home recalls the grand Queen Anne Style designs of the late 19th Century. The foyer offers access to both the bay-windowed dining room and the living area. French doors lead from the living area to a game room, which can easily become a guest room with a private bath. The second floor features two children's bedrooms, each with a walk-in closet and built-in bookcase. The master bedroom has a sitting area with an eleven-foot-high octagon-shaped ceiling. Plenty of linen storage, along with a dressing table, combine with a separate glass-enclosed shower to create a superb master bath. Plans are included for a detached two-car garage.

DESIGN	M9059
BEDROOMS	3
BATHROOMS	3
FIRST FLOOR	1,299 Sq. Ft.
SECOND FLOOR	1,069 Sq. Ft.
TOTAL	2,368 Sq. Ft.
PRICE	A2

FIRST FLOOR

8' Clg. Throughout
Unless Otherwise Noted

WIDTH 54'
DEPTH 40' 2"

SECOND FLOOR

Gameroom
12'-8" x 16'-8"

Bath 2

Porch

French Door

Breakfast
11'-4" x 11'

Util.

French Doors

Family Room
18' x 22'-4"

Kitchen
14' x 12'

8' Clg. Throughout
Unless Otherwise Noted

Foyer

Dining
10' x 11'

FIRST FLOOR

Veranda

Bath

Bedroom 3
10'-8" x 11'

Books

Master Bedroom
18'-4" x 18'-8"

Bath 3

Books

Sitting Area
11' Clg.

Books

Bedroom 2
11'-4" x 12'-8"

SECOND FLOOR

WIDTH 60'
DEPTH 44' 6"

The oval-glass front door of this elegant Queen Anne home opens into the foyer, which showcases the bannistered stairs. The spacious family room has a bay-windowed alcove and a fireplace. French doors lead to the game room, which can easily become guest quarters with a private bath. The kitchen offers a walk-in pantry and abundant cabinet and counter space. Adjacent to the bay-windowed breakfast room is a utility area, with room for the washer, dryer, freezer, and a small counter top with cabinets above. A door from this area can provide access to the two-car detached garage for which plans are included. Upstairs, bedrooms 2 and 3 each have walk-in closets, along with built-in bookcases. The master area, with its sitting alcove and special bath, is the perfect retreat.

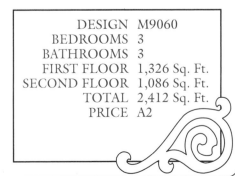

DESIGN	M9060
BEDROOMS	3
BATHROOMS	3
FIRST FLOOR	1,326 Sq. Ft.
SECOND FLOOR	1,086 Sq. Ft.
TOTAL	2,412 Sq. Ft.
PRICE	A2

Double doors open from the two-story foyer to a private study with built-in bookcases and a bay window. The gallery, with decorative wood columns and an arched ceiling, overlooks both the large formal dining and living rooms. French doors open from the living room to the front veranda and the screened porch. A fireplace adds warmth to the breakfast area and the island kitchen. A twelve-foot octagon-shaped ceiling and leaded-glass windows define a cozy sitting area in the master suite. The dressing area, with His and Hers walk-in closets, leads to a luxurious bath. An optional exercise loft and plant shelves complete this elegant master bath. Two additional bedrooms, one with a private deck, share a dressing area and bath.

DESIGN	M9012
BEDROOMS	3
BATHROOMS	2½
FIRST FLOOR	1,357 Sq. Ft.
SECOND FLOOR	1,079 Sq. Ft.
TOTAL	2,436 Sq. Ft.
PRICE	A4

2-Car Garage

9' Clg. Throughout
Unless Otherwise Noted

Util.

Up

Breakfast
10' x 12'

Screened Porch
12' x 10'-4"

Kitchen
10' x 13'

French Doors

Dining
16' x 11'-4"

Living Room
19'-4" x 15'-4"
Coffered Clg.

Gallery

French Doors

French Doors

Foyer

Study
12'-4" x 14'-8"

Books

Veranda

FIRST FLOOR

WIDTH   42' 8"
DEPTH   75'

REAR VIEW

Office
16'-4" x 17'

Optional Second Floor
At Garage
167 Sq. Ft.

Incline Ladder → Bath Below

Exercise Loft
15 x 13

Optional Exercise Loft
228 Sq. Ft.

SECOND FLOOR

Deck

French Doors

Bedroom 2
12' x 11'-4"

Bath 2

Up

Bath

Bedroom 3
12' x 11'-4"
Cathedral Clg.

Foyer
Below

Master Bedroom
12'-4" x 15'

Seat
Books

Balcony

Sitting
Area
12' Clg.

VIEW OF INTERIOR BALCONY

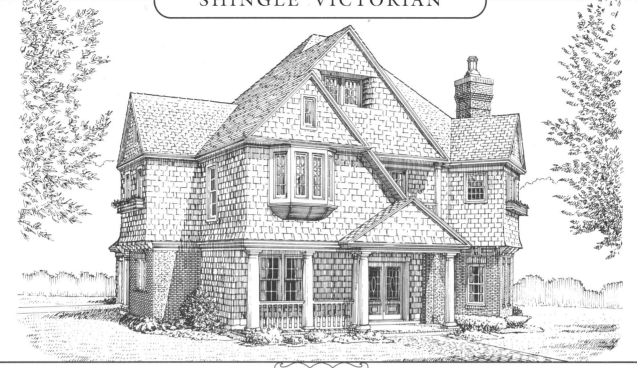

The double leaded-glass doors of this Shingle Style design open into an elegant foyer. The study features raised-panel walls, built-in bookcases and a fireplace. Overlooking the breakfast area and the living room is a spacious kitchen with a walk-in pantry and island cooktop. The living room contains a built-in media center, French doors to the rear porch, and a refreshment bar. Upstairs, the secluded master suite offers a windowed alcove and access to the covered front balcony. The elegant bath utilizes glass block walls for the shower and water closet areas. A corner garden tub and a large walk-in closet complete this area. The additional bedrooms each have unique bay windows and private lavatories.

FIRST FLOOR

SECOND FLOOR

9' Clg. Throughout
Unless Otherwise Noted

DESIGN	M9010
BEDROOMS	3
BATHROOMS	2½
FIRST FLOOR	1,401 Sq. Ft.
SECOND FLOOR	1,189 Sq. Ft.
TOTAL	2,590 Sq. Ft.
PRICE	A4

RIGHT SIDE VIEW

WIDTH 44' 8"
DEPTH 75' 4"

Designed to maximize views to the front, side, and rear outdoor areas, this home utilizes strategically placed windows and an open floor plan. The two-way fireplace and half wall with built-in bookcases separate the living and dining areas. A center work island and walk-in pantry, along with a built-in breakfast nook, are special kitchen amenities. The master suite provides a comfortable retreat with a bay-windowed sitting area and a magnificent bath. Upstairs, a large balcony with a window seat leads to three additional bedrooms. Bedrooms 3 and 4 each feature built-in desks and private dressing areas. Bedroom 2 has a private bath, built-in desk, and French door opening to a rear deck.

SECOND FLOOR

FIRST FLOOR

WIDTH 49' 6"
DEPTH 75'

9' Clg. Throughout

DESIGN	M9011
BEDROOMS	4
BATHROOMS	3½
FIRST FLOOR	1,637 Sq. Ft.
SECOND FLOOR	1,062 Sq. Ft.
TOTAL	2,699 Sq. Ft.
PRICE	A4

Reminiscent of the grand brick Victorians of the late 19th Century, this design features a raised octagon-shaped turret with wraparound veranda, and patterned shingle siding at the gables. The large, two-story living room is perfect for formal or family entertaining, with the breakfast area and kitchen close by. A study with built-in bookcases is perfect for a home office or relaxing reading area. The master suite has a sitting area and a luxurious bath with a glass-enclosed shower, linen storage, and a walk-in closet with full-length mirrored doors. Each of the three upstairs bedrooms has a private lavatory area and ample closet space. The large game room features a cathedral ceiling and a balcony railing overlooking the living room.

FIRST FLOOR

SECOND FLOOR

WIDTH 66'
DEPTH 56' 4"

DESIGN	M9061
BEDROOMS	4
BATHROOMS	3½
FIRST FLOOR	2,087 Sq. Ft.
SECOND FLOOR	1,150 Sq. Ft.
TOTAL	3,237 Sq. Ft.
PRICE	A3

SECOND FLOOR

Deck

French Door

Living Room Below or Optional Gameroom
17' x 17'
300 Sq. Ft.

Balcony

Bedroom 3
12'-8" x 11'

Linen

Bath 2

Bath 3

Foyer Below

Bedroom 2
12' x 13'

Bedroom 4
12'-8" x 13'

8' Clg. Throughout Second Floor
Unless Otherwise Noted

WIDTH 62' 6"
DEPTH 65' 4"

Mirrored Doors

Bath
Cathedral Clg.

Books

Linen

Master Bedroom
14' x 17'

Living Room
18' x 20'
19' Clg.

Porch

French Door

Wet Bar

Family Room
20' x 13'-4"

Util.

Breakfast
11' x 11'

Kitchen
11' x 13'

Foyer

Up

Sitting Area

Books

Study
11'-4" x 14'-4"

Dining
11'-4" x 14'-4"

10' Clg. Throughout First Floor
Unless Otherwise Noted

FIRST FLOOR

Decorative shingle siding and a dominant front veranda create a charming turn-of-the-century exterior. The magnificent foyer offers a view of the two-story living area with floor-to-ceiling glass at the rear. A raised walkway provides a dramatic entry to the master suite with a cozy sitting area. The kitchen features a walk-in pantry and boxed-out window at the sink. The family room has a bay-window area and French doors opening to the covered porch. A hallway leads to a two-car detached garage, for which plans are included. Upstairs, a balcony walkway leads to bedroom 4 with a private bath. Bedrooms 2 and 3 have ample closet space and a shared bath with separate dressing areas. The plans offer an optional 17' x 17' game area above the living room.

DESIGN	M9062
BEDROOMS	4
BATHROOMS	3½
FIRST FLOOR	2,254 Sq. Ft.
SECOND FLOOR	928 Sq. Ft.
TOTAL	3,182 Sq. Ft.
PRICE	A5

QUEEN ANNE

8' Clg. Throughout Second Floor
Unless Otherwise Noted

The living area of this spectacular Queen Anne Style home features a fireplace and a bay-windowed alcove. The centrally located kitchen overlooks a dining area with full-length windows and a French door. The master bedroom has a large walk-in closet and French doors opening to the rear veranda. The master bath provides additional closet space, along with a glass-enclosed shower and an oval tub in an octagon-shaped alcove. Upstairs, French doors open into a game room. Bedroom 2 has a walk-in closet and a ten-foot sloped ceiling. Bedroom 3 also has a walk-in closet and a raised octagon-shaped ceiling. Plans are included for a detached two-car garage and an optional screened porch.

WIDTH 40' 4"
DEPTH 62' 10"

SECOND FLOOR

FIRST FLOOR

9' Clg. Throughout First Floor
Unless Otherwise Noted

DESIGN   M9063
BEDROOMS   3
BATHROOMS 2½
FIRST FLOOR   1,236 Sq. Ft.
SECOND FLOOR   835 Sq. Ft.
TOTAL   2,071 Sq. Ft.
PRICE   A4

REAR VIEW

FIRST FLOOR

French Door

Breakfast
10' x 10'

Desk

Kitchen
12' x 13'

Family Room
16' x 20'

Wine Rack

Hutch

Wet Bar

Dining
17' x 12'

Books

Study
14' x 12'

French Doors

Foyer

Parlor
12' x 16'

Veranda

9' Clg. Throughout
Unless Otherwise Noted

French Door

SECOND FLOOR

Deck

French Door

Linen   Planter

Bath

Master Bedroom
16' x 15'

Util.

Bath 2

Bedroom 2
14' x 12'
13' Clg.

Foyer Below

Bedroom 3
13' x 11'

Study
Alcove

Bedroom 4
12' x 16'

**LEFT SIDE
VIEW**

WIDTH 47' 10"
DEPTH 59' 2"

The angled entry opens to a grand foyer and a formal parlor with expansive windows and a French door leading to the side yard. Double French doors open from the foyer to the large study with bookcases and full-length windows. The spacious family room features a fireplace and a wet bar. The kitchen, with a work island and abundant cabinet space, overlooks the octagon-shaped breakfast room. Upstairs, the master bedroom has French doors which open onto a rear deck. Three additional bedrooms each have walk-in closets. Bedroom 2 has a thirteen-foot octagon-shaped ceiling, while bedroom 4 offers a cozy alcove with built-in desk and shuttered opening to the foyer. Plans for a two-car detached garage are included.

DESIGN   M9014
BEDROOMS   4
BATHROOMS   2½
FIRST FLOOR   1,565 Sq. Ft.
SECOND FLOOR   1,598 Sq. Ft.
TOTAL   3,163 Sq. Ft.
PRICE   A5

An oval-glass front door with side-lights opens into a raised foyer, which overlooks the formal dining and living areas. The bookcase-lined alcove at the front of the living room is a perfect reading area. The kitchen features a walk-in pantry, center island with vegetable sink, and an abundance of counter and cabinet space. The master retreat features a special bath with glass-enclosed shower, oval tub, and a dressing alcove with mirrored closet doors. The centrally located staircase is both elegant and practical. Upstairs, bedrooms 3 and 4 offer private lavatory areas, while sharing a bath. Bedroom 2 has a personal bath, walk-in closet and built-in desk. The balcony has three leaded-glass windows above a window seat.

9' Clg. Throughout First Floor

FIRST FLOOR

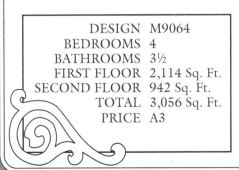

SECOND FLOOR

8' Clg. Throughout Second Floor

DESIGN M9064
BEDROOMS 4
BATHROOMS 3½
FIRST FLOOR 2,114 Sq. Ft.
SECOND FLOOR 942 Sq. Ft.
TOTAL 3,056 Sq. Ft.
PRICE A3

WIDTH 62'
DEPTH 65' 6"

QUEEN ANNE

Game Area
12' x 12'
10' Clg.

French Door

French Door

Family Room
16' x 16'

French Doors

Breakfast
11' x 10'

Living Room
19' x 18'

Media Center

Books

Kitchen
16' x 14'

Wet Bar

Books

French Doors

Study
14' x 15'

Books

Foyer

Dining
12' x 16'

Niche

Veranda

FIRST FLOOR

9' Clg. Throughout
First Floor Unless
Otherwise Noted

8' Clg. Throughout Second Floor
Unless Otherwise Noted

The dramatic two-story foyer leads to the study and living room, both with built-in cabinets and bookcases. The family room features a game table area with full-length windows, along with a wet bar and media center. The kitchen is a gourmet's delight with an island cooktop, walk-in pantry, and an oven inset in brick. French doors open onto the rear porch from the breakfast area and the family room. Upstairs, bedrooms 2 and 3 each have walk-in closets and private dressing areas. A ten-foot octagon-shaped ceiling and leaded-glass windows define a cozy sitting area in the master suite. A two-car detached garage design is included in the plans.

Mirrored Doors

Window Seat

Bedroom 3
13' x 12'

Linen

Bath
10' Clg.

Util.

Linen

Balcony

Bath 2

WIDTH 52' 8"
DEPTH 57' 8"

Master Bedroom
18' x 15'

Books

Foyer Below

Bedroom 2
12' x 14'

Sitting Area
10' Clg.

SECOND FLOOR

DESIGN	M9065
BEDROOMS	3
BATHROOMS	2½
FIRST FLOOR	1,907 Sq. Ft.
SECOND FLOOR	1,367 Sq. Ft.
TOTAL	3,274 Sq. Ft.
PRICE	A3

SHINGLE VICTORIAN

9' Clg. Throughout Unless Otherwise Noted

The leaded-glass front door opens into a spacious foyer, which offers a view of the formal dining room. The living room features a fireplace with cabinets on one side and a window seat on the other. A library alcove, with windows above a desk and a four-foot bookcase below the stairs, connects the living and family areas. The kitchen features an island cooktop, an angled window and sink, and a French door leading to the side veranda. Adjacent to the kitchen is a staircase to an optional game room or living quarters. The master suite offers a private media center with built-in seating and cabinets for audio and video equipment. The two additional bedrooms each have closets and private bathrooms.

DESIGN	M9066
BEDROOMS	3
BATHROOMS	4
FIRST FLOOR	1,353 Sq. Ft.
SECOND FLOOR	1,279 Sq. Ft.
GAME ROOM	311 Sq. Ft.
(OPTIONAL)	
TOTAL	2,943 Sq. Ft.
PRICE	A4

FIRST FLOOR

WIDTH 55' 6"
DEPTH 66' 8"

2-Car Garage

Util. 8' x 6'

French Door

Bath 2

Pantry

Nook

Built-in Breakfast Shelf

Built-in Table

Porch

French Door

Window Seat

Family Room 21'-4" x 15'-4" Coffered Clg.

Media Center

Kitchen 17' x 12'

Desk

Library Alcove

Recessed Bookcase

French Doors

Dining 14'-4" x 12'-4"

Foyer

Living Room 16'-8" x 11'

Veranda

Books Seat

First Floor

Optional Gameroom 10'-8" x 26' 9' Clg.

6'-2" Wall

Bath 4

Linen

Bedroom 3 12' x 13'-4"

Bath

6'-6" Wall

Bath 3

Books Desk

Linen

5'-6" Wall

Bedroom 2 10'-8" x 15'-4"

Built-in Seating

Master Bedroom 18'-4" x 11'

Media 9' x 9' Desk

Seat

Second Floor

SECOND FLOOR

REAR VIEW

FIRST FLOOR

9' Clg. Throughout

SECOND FLOOR

The wraparound veranda and simple lines give this home an unassuming elegance that is characteristic of its Folk Victorian heritage. Opening directly to the formal dining room, the two-story foyer offers extra space for large dinner parties. French doors lead to the study with a cozy fireplace. The private master suite features a corner garden tub, glass-enclosed shower, and a walk-in closet. Overlooking the family room and built-in breakfast nook is the central kitchen. A rear staircase provides convenient access to the second floor from the family room. The balcony provides a view of the foyer below and the Palladian window. Three additional bedrooms complete this exquisite home.

DESIGN	M9067
BEDROOMS	4
BATHROOMS	3½
FIRST FLOOR	1,999 Sq. Ft.
SECOND FLOOR	933 Sq. Ft.
TOTAL	2,932 Sq. Ft.
PRICE	A4

WIDTH 79' 8"
DEPTH 59'

REAR VIEW

The raised turret with a wraparound veranda and front gable with decorative shingle siding dominate the facade of this Queen Anne Style home. An alcove is situated at the front of the living room. The country-style kitchen opens directly to the breakfast area. The secluded master bedroom features a master bath with His and Hers walk-in closets, a custom octagon-shaped tub and separate shower. A rear door at the utility room opens to the back porch, which can be connected with an optional covered walk to the detached two-car garage, for which plans are included. Upstairs, three bedrooms share a large, well-planned bathroom.

WIDTH 59' 8"
DEPTH 57' 8"

8' Clg. Throughout
Second Floor
Unless Otherwise Noted

SECOND FLOOR

Bedroom 4
13' x 12'

Bath 2

Bedroom 2
10' x 17'
10' Clg.

Bedroom 3
11' x 14'

Master Bedroom
17'-8" x 13'-4"

Porch

Breakfast
11' x 14'

Util.

French Doors

Kitchen
16' x 12'

Bath

Living Room
17' x 20'

Pantry

Wet Bar

Dining
12' x 14'

Library
11' x 9'

Books

Veranda

10' Clg. Throughout First Floor

FIRST FLOOR

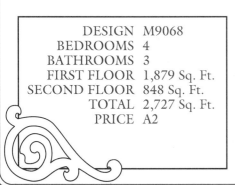

DESIGN   M9068
BEDROOMS   4
BATHROOMS   3
FIRST FLOOR   1,879 Sq. Ft.
SECOND FLOOR   848 Sq. Ft.
TOTAL   2,727 Sq. Ft.
PRICE   A2

Storage

Util.

2-Car Garage

French Door
Breakfast
11'-4" x 11'-4"

Wet Bar

Kitchen
11' x 15'

Dining
14' x 15'

Family Room
17'-8" x 16'-8"

Books/Media Center

French Doors

Foyer

Living Room
18'-4" x 13'-8"

Display Niche

Veranda

FIRST FLOOR

Optional
Loft
12' x 11'-4"
136 Sq. Ft.

9' Clg. Throughout
Unless Otherwise Noted

Bedroom 2
12' x 15'
Cathedral Clg.

Linen

Bath 2

Bath 3

Bedroom 3
11'-8" x 11'-8"

Balcony

Linen

Bath

Barrel Clg.
Above Bath

Bedroom 4
12' x 16'-8"

Bath 4

Up To Optional
Exercise Room

Sauna

Master Bedroom
18'-4" x 13'-8"

Balcony

Foyer
Below

Sitting Area
11'-4" x 11'-4"
Vaulted Clg.

Balcony

SECOND FLOOR

REAR VIEW

Queen Anne Style homes of the late 19th Century feature some of the most elaborate and intricate construction and detailing ever witnessed in residential design. Reminiscent of these grand homes, this design offers some of the same distinctive characteristics: the patterned shingle siding, ornate spindlework, porch balustrades and the curved windows in the raised turrets. Leaded-glass doors open to a truly grand foyer with elegant staircase to a balcony above. The living room has a sitting area and French doors to a side veranda. Upstairs is the private master suite with luxurious bath, and three additional bedrooms, each with private bath and walk-in closet.

DESIGN	M9017
BEDROOMS	4
BATHROOMS	4½
FIRST FLOOR	1,617 Sq. Ft.
SECOND FLOOR	1,818 Sq. Ft.
OPTIONAL LOFT	136 Sq. Ft.
TOTAL	3,435 Sq. Ft.
PRICE	A5

WIDTH 53'
DEPTH 64' 8"

This home offers the essential characteristics of the Queen Anne Style—a raised turret and ornate spindlework at the veranda—but adds the practicality of a brick-veneer first floor. Inside, the living room has a bay-windowed alcove and a massive brick fireplace. Full-length windows on two sides of the breakfast room offer an expansive view of the rear yard. Matching sets of French doors open from the gallery and the master bedroom to the porch. An optional two-way fireplace separates the master bedroom and bath. Upstairs, bedrooms 3 and 4 each have private lavatories and walk-in closets. The game room has an optional fireplace and wet bar. Plans for a two-car detached garage are included.

FIRST FLOOR

9' Clg. Throughout First Floor

8' Clg. Throughout Second Floor
Unless Otherwise Noted

SECOND FLOOR

DESIGN M9069
BEDROOMS 4
BATHROOMS 3½
FIRST FLOOR 1,937 Sq. Ft.
SECOND FLOOR 1,410 Sq. Ft.
TOTAL 3,347 Sq. Ft.
PRICE A5

WIDTH 53'
DEPTH 54'

FIRST FLOOR

Bath
Porch
Util.
Master Bedroom
16'-4" x 17'
French Doors
Veranda
Breakfast
10' x 14'
1/2 Bath
Kitchen
12' x 13'
Gallery
Study
11' x 13'-4'
Up
Wet Bar
Books
Wine Rack
French Doors
Dining
16' x 12'-8'
Living Room
16' x 23'
Raised Foyer
French Doors
Veranda

10' Clg. Throughout First Floor

WIDTH 54' 4"
DEPTH 75'

8' Clg. Throughout Second Floor

Plant Shelf
Bedroom 2
15' x 10'
Balcony
Bath 3
Bedroom 3
13' x 15–4'
Window Seats
Bath 2
Media Center
Up To Optional Third Floor
Bedroom 4
13' x 13'
Foyer Below
Gameroom
16' x 23'

SECOND FLOOR

LEFT
SIDE VIEW

This Victorian-inspired home, with its wide veranda and generous use of expansive windows and French doors, can take advantage of a building site that offers views in every direction. The raised foyer directly overlooks the formal dining room and the living area. Special features like the built-in bookcases in the study, the wet bar serving both living area and gallery, and an island kitchen with attached breakfast room and walk-in pantry make the gathering and working areas complete. Note the spacious bedrooms—master with whirlpool bath on the first floor and three additional bedrooms upstairs. Also upstairs is a game room with media center and fireplace. A staircase leads to an optional third-floor area. A two-car detached garage plan is included with this design.

DESIGN	M9013
BEDROOMS	4
BATHROOMS	3½
FIRST FLOOR	2,385 Sq. Ft.
SECOND FLOOR	1,467 Sq. Ft.
TOTAL	3,852 Sq. Ft.
PRICE	A5

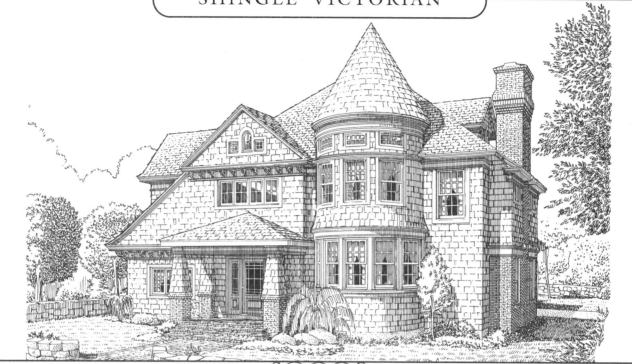

Towards the end of the Victorian era, a new style began to emerge along the Eastern Seaboard. Later referred to as the Shingle Style, these new designs were influenced by the Colonial Revival and Queen Anne homes. Often incorporating diverse architectural elements, the shingle siding is one of the common elements of this style. With its cantilevered gable sloping in a gentle curve to the first floor, and a raised turret, this design is representative of this late 19th-Century style. Besides the living and dining rooms with coffered ceilings, the home boasts a study with curved walls, central gallery and family room with sunken media center. The island kitchen has an adjacent breakfast booth. Upstairs is a grand master suite and three additional bedrooms.

FIRST FLOOR

SECOND FLOOR

9' Clg. Throughout Unless Otherwise Noted

DESIGN	M9016
BEDROOMS	4
BATHROOMS	4½
FIRST FLOOR	1,812 Sq. Ft.
SECOND FLOOR	1,997 Sq. Ft.
TOTAL	3,809 Sq. Ft.
PRICE	A5

WIDTH 49' 2"
DEPTH 71' 8"

REAR VIEW

FIRST FLOOR

9' Clg. Throughout First and Second Floor
Unless Otherwise Noted

SECOND FLOOR

WIDTH 65' 4"
DEPTH 56'

**DETACHED
3-CAR GARAGE**

Reminiscent of the fashionable summer homes of Newport, Cape Cod, this home typifies the Shingle Style with its wide verandas, shingled surfaces, Palladian window, and circular tower. The library features a built-in bookcase and circular study. To the left of the fireplace in the game room is a brick archway with built-in media center. To the right, a matching brick archway leads to the adjoining pub and walk-in wet bar. Windows surround the spacious kitchen. The second-floor master suite includes two oversized walk-in closets and a luxury bath. Three additional bedrooms and two baths, as well as a multi-purpose media room, are also on the second floor. Plans for a three-car detached garage with second-floor living quarters are included.

DESIGN M9070
BEDROOMS 4
BATHROOMS 4½
FIRST FLOOR 2,083 Sq. Ft.
SECOND FLOOR 1,938 Sq. Ft.
TOTAL 4,021 Sq. Ft.
PRICE A6

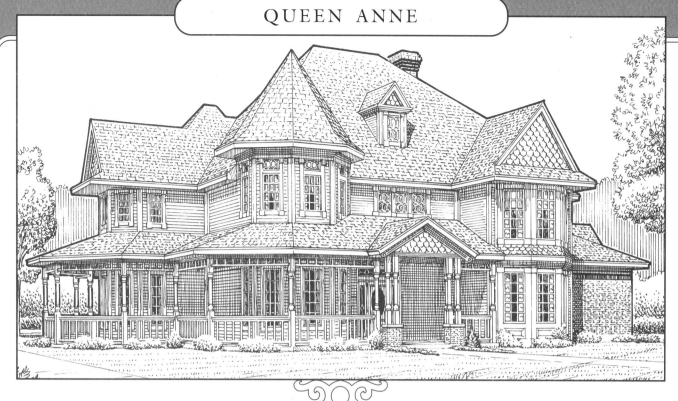

This lovely Queen Anne Style design has all the amenities you would expect in such a grand home. The raised foyer overlooks the formal dining room and living area, and provides access to a bay-windowed study and the secluded master suite with a sitting area, fireplace, and amenity-laden bath. Next to the large kitchen and breakfast area is a laundry room, and a special home office or hobby room. Upstairs, bedrooms 2 and 3 each have walk-in closets and separate dressing areas. Bedroom 4 features a built-in desk and a private dressing area. Triple French doors open from the balcony to a spectacular game room. Plans for a two-car detached garage are included.

FIRST FLOOR

10' Clg. Throughout First Floor

SECOND FLOOR

8' Clg. Throughout Second Floor
Unless Otherwise Noted

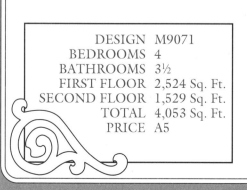

DESIGN	M9071
BEDROOMS	4
BATHROOMS	3½
FIRST FLOOR	2,524 Sq. Ft.
SECOND FLOOR	1,529 Sq. Ft.
TOTAL	4,053 Sq. Ft.
PRICE	A5

WIDTH 75' 8"
DEPTH 62' 4"

2-Car Garage

Garage/Stor.

Porch

French Door

Breakfast
13'-8" x 11'-4"

Courtyard

Living Room
19' x 23'

French Doors

Gallery

Kitchen
13'-8" x 15'

Telephone Booth

French Door

Bath 4

Books

Foyer

Dining
12'-4" x 17'

Veranda

Study
11'-4" x 12'-4"

FIRST FLOOR

8' Clg. Throughout
Unless Otherwise Noted

WIDTH 53' 6"
DEPTH 82' 8"

Bath 3

Window Seat

Bedroom 3
13' x 16'
Sloped Clg.

Down To Courtyard

Stor.

Util.

Up To Attic

Her Bath

His Bath

Balcony

Bath 2

Master Bedroom
18' x 13'
10' Step-Up Clg.

Foyer Below

Bedroom 2
13'-8" x 14'

Sitting Area
11' x 14'

SECOND FLOOR

Balance and symmetry, along with elaborate gingerbread detailing, highlight this Queen Anne Style design. Inside, the living room, kitchen, and breakfast area are ideal for relaxing or entertaining. Accessible from the foyer and living room, the study has a walk-in storage area, and built-in bookcases. It can double as a guest room. From the breakfast area, rear stairs lead to the second floor. Bedroom 3 can be a secluded area for an older child. The conveniently located utility room not only offers plenty of space for the laundry, but also has room for various other hobbies or projects. Leading to the master suite is a balcony that overlooks the dramatic foyer and stairs on one side, and the courtyard on the other.

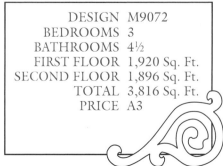

DESIGN	M9072
BEDROOMS	3
BATHROOMS	4½
FIRST FLOOR	1,920 Sq. Ft.
SECOND FLOOR	1,896 Sq. Ft.
TOTAL	3,816 Sq. Ft.
PRICE	A3

SECOND FLOOR

Books/Media Center

Gameroom
16'-4" x 13'-8"

Deck

Bedroom 4
18' x 10'-8"

Bath 3

Books

Balcony

Bath 4

Bedroom 2
15' x 16'-8"

Foyer Below

Bedroom 3
15' x 14'

9' Clg. Throughout Second Floor

2-Car Garage

Bath 2

Util.

Mirrored Doors

Bath
Cathedral Clg.

Books/Media Center

Garden Room
14' x 10'

Breakfast
18'-8" x 10'

WIDTH 74' 8"
DEPTH 83' 4"

Linen

Living Room
19'-4" x 20'

Kitchen
15' x 13'

Master Bedroom
15' x 15'

Foyer

Books

Dining
15' x 14'

Sitting Area

Study
15' x 13'-4"

FIRST FLOOR

Veranda

10' Clg. Throughout First Floor

All of the essential elements of the Queen Anne Style are present on the exterior of this gracious and inviting home. However, once inside, it immediately becomes obvious that this design reflects the lifestyles of today. The living room features built-in bookcases and a media center, and an expansive window treatment. The optional garden room can be fully enclosed for all-weather enjoyment, or left open as a covered porch. The island kitchen overlooks a bay-windowed breakfast area. The master suite has a sitting alcove with leaded-glass transom window. An enormous bath showcases an oversized garden tub. Upstairs, bedrooms 3 and 4 share a large bath. The game room has an optional fireplace and built-in bookcases and media cabinets.

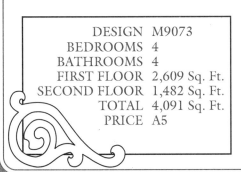

DESIGN	M9073
BEDROOMS	4
BATHROOMS	4
FIRST FLOOR	2,609 Sq. Ft.
SECOND FLOOR	1,482 Sq. Ft.
TOTAL	4,091 Sq. Ft.
PRICE	A5

FIRST FLOOR

2-Car Garage

Storage

T.V.

Sunken Media Center 11' x 12'

French Doors

Seating

Breakfast 10' x 10'

28' High Wall

Down

Utility

Cabinets

Dining 13'-4" x 14'-8"

Kitchen 12' x 12'

Family Room 18'-4" x 15'-4"

Gallery

32' High Wall

French Doors

Books/Cabinets

Living Room 13'-4" x 17'

Study 13'-4" x 15'

Foyer

Porch

9' Clg. Throughout
Unless Otherwise Noted

SECOND FLOOR

Bedroom 2 13'-4" x 12'-4"

Bath 2

Laundry

Up To Optional 3rd Floor

Deck

Bedroom 3 13'-4" x 12'-4"

French Doors

Bath 3

Down

Master Bedroom 18'-4" x 15'-4"

Linen

Marble Pedestal

Seat W/Storage

Down

Dressing Table

Bedroom 4 13'-4" x 12'-8"

Foyer Below

Bath

Gazebo Clg. At Tub

Exercise Room 11'-4" x 8' Cathedral Clg.

Linen

Seat

Seat

WIDTH 59' 4"
DEPTH 72' 8"

During the middle of the 19th Century, homes were inspired by Gothic Revival details. Later, turned posts and delicate spindles were added to the porches, along with eave brackets and ornate cornice trim. Referred to as Folk Victorians, these homes were built until the beginning of the 20th Century. As authentic as the exterior of this design is, the interior offers a wealth of luxury and elegance. Note formal and informal living areas, the centrally located kitchen, plentiful built-ins and ample storage. The secluded master suite with exercise room is beyond compare. Three additional bedrooms and a laundry room complete the second floor. A staircase leads to an optional 14' x 39' third floor area.

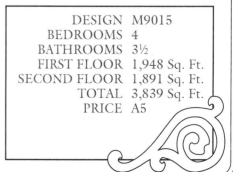

REAR VIEW

DESIGN	M9015
BEDROOMS	4
BATHROOMS	3½
FIRST FLOOR	1,948 Sq. Ft.
SECOND FLOOR	1,891 Sq. Ft.
TOTAL	3,839 Sq. Ft.
PRICE	A5

A raised front gable with decorative shingles and a porch with ornate posts and brackets recall the simple charm of the Folk Victorian cottages built throughout this country at the turn of the century. The family room focuses on a fireplace with flanking full-width windows. The country-style kitchen offers ample dining space with its large bay window. The master bedroom features a ten-foot ceiling, a private dressing area, and a walk-in closet. The laundry room is conveniently located close to bedrooms 2 and 3. Plans for a detached two-car garage are included.

Bedroom 3
11' x 12'-4"

Bedroom 2
10' x 10'

Kitchen
10' x 10'

Dining
10' x 10'

Util.

Bath 2

Family Room
14' x 19'-4"
10' Clg.

Bath

Master Bedroom
11'-4" x 17'
10' Clg.

Porch

8' Clg. Throughout Unless Otherwise Noted

DESIGN   M9032
BEDROOMS   3
BATHROOMS   2
SQUARE FOOTAGE 1,358
PRICE   A1

WIDTH   43' 4"
DEPTH   40' 2"

Bedroom 3
12'-4" x 11'-4"

Bedroom 2
12'-4" x 10'-4"

Util.

Porch

Dining
10' x 13'

Bath 2

Bath

Family Room
15'-4" x 20'
10' Clg.

Kitchen
10' x 12'

Desk

Master Bedroom
12'-4" x 17'-8"

Porch

8' Clg. Throughout Unless Otherwise Noted

WIDTH 44' 8"
DEPTH 54' 2"

While the roof line and porch details are reminiscent of a turn-of-the-century Farmhouse, the majority of the exterior is actually low-maintenance brick veneer. The family room, with its ten-foot ceiling, is a perfect area for relaxing or entertaining. A French door opens from the bay-windowed dining area to a covered porch. The efficiently designed kitchen has a built-in desk with a box window and lots of cabinet space. Located next to bedrooms 2 and 3, the laundry room has space for a freezer or additional storage. Plans are included for a detached two-car garage.

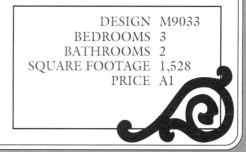

DESIGN M9033
BEDROOMS 3
BATHROOMS 2
SQUARE FOOTAGE 1,528
PRICE A1

This economical Farmhouse design offers a practical floor plan with some exciting surprises. The dining area is filled with natural light from a full-length bay window at the front of the house, while the kitchen area enjoys plenty of sun and light from the bay window over the sink. A nine-foot gambrel ceiling and fireplace add to the coziness of the family room. The private master bedroom has both a walk-in closet and a small linen closet. The laundry room is conveniently located next to bedrooms 2 and 3. Plans for a detached two-car garage are included.

WIDTH 36' 10"
DEPTH 57' 6"

Bath

Master Bedroom
13'-8" x 11'-8"

Bedroom 2
10' x 11'-4"

Bath
2

Util.

Family Room
16' x 17'
9' Gambrel Clg.

Bedroom 3
13' x 10'

Foyer

Kitchen
16' x 9'

Porch

Dining
11' x 10'

8' Clg. Throughout Unless Otherwise Noted

DESIGN	M9035
BEDROOMS	3
BATHROOMS	2
SQUARE FOOTAGE	1,341
PRICE	A1

Bedroom 3
15'-4" x 11'-8"

Bedroom 2
10'-8" x 11'-8"

Family Room
17'-4" x 20'
10' Gambrel Clg.

Util.

Porch

French Door

Bath 2

Bath

Breakfast
14' x 10'

Kitchen
13' x 12'

Dining
11'-8" x 12'

Foyer

Master Bedroom
16' x 15'
9' Clg.

Porch

8' Clg. Throughout Unless Otherwise Noted

WIDTH 54' 2"
DEPTH 59' 6"

With its front bay window, wrap-around porch, and shutters, this home possesses both country charm and elegance. The foyer opens to a formal dining room, and a short hall that leads to the secluded master bedroom. The master bath features plenty of linen storage, along with His and Hers walk-in closets. The kitchen overlooks a large bay-windowed breakfast area and also offers a practical 42-inch-high eating bar. Full-length windows flanking a brick fireplace and a ten-foot gambrel ceiling are highlights of the family room. Bedrooms 2 and 3 each have large walk-in closets. Plans for a detached two-car garage are included.

DESIGN	M9039
BEDROOMS	3
BATHROOMS	2
SQUARE FOOTAGE	1,978
PRICE	A1

This practical and rather economical one-story Farmhouse design offers a wraparound front porch with ornate posts and railing. The living room not only features a ten-foot ceiling, but also offers expansive windows and a built-in bookcase. The kitchen, with its walk-in pantry, overlooks a large bay-windowed dining area. A cathedral ceiling enhances the master bedroom. His and Hers walk-in closets and a large linen closet are focal points of the master bath. Plans for a two-car detached garage are included.

DESIGN M9038
BEDROOMS 3
BATHROOMS 2
SQUARE FOOTAGE 1,659
PRICE A1

WIDTH 63' 4"
DEPTH 37' 10"

Bedroom 3
13'-8" x 10'

Bath
2

Bedroom 2
10' x 11'

Util.

Kitchen
11' x 11'

French Door

Dining
11' x 11'
Vaulted Clg.

Hutch

Bath

**Master
Bedroom**
11'-8" x 20'
10' Clg.

Living Room
17' x 20'
10' Clg.

Books

Linen

Porch

8' Clg. Throughout
Unless Otherwise Noted

WIDTH 48' 10"
DEPTH 46' 10"

Boasting an efficient floor plan with plenty of closet space, this Farmhouse is rather economical to build. The simple roof design and well-proportioned bay window and front porch, which are far less costly than many Farmhouse designs, allow extras such as the ten-foot ceilings in the master bedroom and the living room, and the unique "gazebo" vaulted ceiling in the dining area. Optional bookcases are located on each side of the fireplace. The laundry room is conveniently located near the bedrooms. The sides and part of the rear of the home are brick veneer, providing for much less maintenance and painting. Plans for a two-car detached garage are included with this design.

DESIGN	M9007
BEDROOMS	3
BATHROOMS	2
SQUARE FOOTAGE	1,669
PRICE	A1

Designed for casual living inside and out, this one-story Farmhouse is an ideal family home. The family room features a ten-foot ceiling and a corner fireplace. An enormous dining area can handle even the largest family dinners. The large rear porch is perfect for outdoor entertaining. The laundry room is conveniently located near the three bedrooms. His and Hers walk-in closets and twin lavatories are part of the luxurious master bath. Plans for a 24' x 24' detached garage are included with this design.

Master Bedroom
14'-4" x 15'-4"

Bath

Linen

Bedroom 3
11'-4" x 13'-8"

Porch
25'-4" x 8'

Util.

Dining
17' x 11'-4"

Bath 2

Family Room
17' x 21'-8"
10' Clg.

Kitchen
11' x 13'

Foyer

Bedroom 2
12'-4" x 10'-8"
10' Clg.

Porch

8' Clg. Throughout
Unless Otherwise Noted

DESIGN	M9006
BEDROOMS	3
BATHROOMS	2
SQUARE FOOTAGE	1,772
PRICE	A1

WIDTH 51' 2"
DEPTH 52' 10"

Porch

Breakfast
9' x 8'

French Door

Bath

Util.

Window Seat

Master
Bedroom
12' x 15'
10' Gambrel Clg.

Kitchen
10' x 12'

Family Room
16' x 21'

Dining
11' x 13'

Porch

8' Clg. Throughout
Unless Otherwise Noted

FIRST FLOOR

With its brick-veneer exterior, dormer windows and wraparound porch, this home is a blend of the early 1900s Farmhouse and the Prairie Style. Corner box windows provide a cozy sitting area next to the fireplace in the family room. The efficient kitchen overlooks the breakfast area with its full-length windows. A French door opens to a large covered porch. Double doors open to the master bedroom with a ten-foot gambrel ceiling. The bath features mirrored closet doors and double lavatories. Upstairs, there are two bedrooms, each with dormer window alcoves and sloping ceilings. Plans for a two-car detached garage are included.

Bath 2

HVAC

Bedroom 2
10' x 12'

Bedroom 3
10' x 12'

SECOND FLOOR

WIDTH 44'
DEPTH 45'

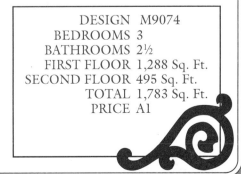

DESIGN M9074
BEDROOMS 3
BATHROOMS 2½
FIRST FLOOR 1,288 Sq. Ft.
SECOND FLOOR 495 Sq. Ft.
TOTAL 1,783 Sq. Ft.
PRICE A1

The timeless beauty and practicality of the wraparound veranda give this Farmhouse a casual, yet distinctive appearance. The efficiently designed kitchen opens to a light-filled breakfast area with full-length windows and a French door that leads to the veranda. The master suite offers His and Hers lavatories and a large walk-in closet. Upstairs, optional skylights provide plenty of natural light to the balcony. Two bedrooms share a bath that has separate bathing and dressing areas. Plans for a two-car detached garage are included.

French Door

Master Bedroom 12' x 13'-8"

Bath

Util.

Breakfast 10' x 10'

Kitchen 11' x 12'

French Door

Living Room 16' x 17'

Dining 11' x 12'

Veranda

8' Clg. Throughout

FIRST FLOOR

Skylights

Bedroom 3 10'-8" x 13'

Bath 2

Bedroom 2 11' x 13'

Slope

Linen

Slope

SECOND FLOOR

DESIGN	M9003
BEDROOMS	3
BATHROOMS	2½
FIRST FLOOR	1,244 Sq. Ft.
SECOND FLOOR	551 Sq. Ft.
TOTAL	1,795 Sq. Ft.
PRICE	A4

WIDTH 46'
DEPTH 38' 8"

Veranda

French Doors

Breakfast
10' x 10'

Bath

Planter

Util.

Master Bedroom
13' x 13'-4"

½ Bath

Kitchen
12' x 10'

Living Room
17'-4" x 17'

Dining
12'-4" x 14'

Foyer

Veranda

WIDTH 53'
DEPTH 45' 4"

FIRST FLOOR

9' Clg. Throughout

The wraparound veranda and simple, uncluttered lines give this home an unassuming elegance that is characteristic of its Farmhouse heritage. The kitchen overlooks an octagon-shaped breakfast room with full-length windows and a French door that opens to the rear veranda. An exceptional master bedroom provides plenty of closet space and an elegant bath. Located within an oversized bay window is a garden tub with adjacent planter and glass-enclosed shower. Upstairs, two bedrooms share a bath with separate dressing and bathing areas. The balcony sitting area is a perfect playroom or study area. Plans for a two-car garage are included.

Sitting Area
10' x 10'-4"

SECOND FLOOR

Bedroom 2
11'-4" x 15'-8"

Bedroom 3
12' x 14'-4"

Bath

DESIGN M9001
BEDROOMS 3
BATHROOMS 2½
FIRST FLOOR 1,308 Sq. Ft.
SECOND FLOOR 751 Sq. Ft.
TOTAL 2,059 Sq. Ft.
PRICE A4

The symmetry and grace of the turn-of-the-century Farmhouse is captured in this design. The veranda provides plenty of shade for outdoor activities. Inside, the kitchen with center island work counter opens to the breakfast area with a full-length bay window. The master bedroom features a walk-in closet and abundant linen storage. A corner tub and glass-enclosed shower highlight the bath. An optional French door allows access to a swimming pool, or possibly a private spa. Upstairs, the balcony overlooks the living room below. Two bedrooms each have walk-in closets and private dressing areas. Plans for a detached two-car garage are included.

FIRST FLOOR

8' Clg. Throughout Unless Otherwise Noted

WIDTH 57' 4"
DEPTH 37' 8"

SECOND FLOOR

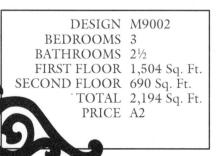

DESIGN M9002
BEDROOMS 3
BATHROOMS 2½
FIRST FLOOR 1,504 Sq. Ft.
SECOND FLOOR 690 Sq. Ft.
TOTAL 2,194 Sq. Ft.
PRICE A2

8' Clg. Throughout

FIRST FLOOR

Porch
French Door
Living Room
17' x 23'
Util.
Bath
Linen
Balcony Above
Breakfast
15' x 10'
Master Bedroom
15' x 17'
Dining
11' x 13'
Kitchen
11' x 16'
Foyer
32" High Wall
Veranda

The wraparound veranda of this Farmhouse design offers a shaded outdoor living area. Inside, an efficient floor plan provides plenty of open living areas. The foyer and formal dining room are separated by a 32-inch-high wall, while the kitchen opens directly to a spacious breakfast area. A small rear porch can be connected by a breezeway to the detached garage (plan included). The highlight of this home is the living room. A center fireplace with tall glass on each side soars to the top of the cathedral ceiling, while a balcony opens from the game room above. A French door opens to the rear porch. The master suite features His and Hers walk-in closets and abundant linen storage. Each upstairs bedroom offers a built-in desk or window seat.

SECOND FLOOR

Living Room Below
Cathedral Clg.
Balcony
Bedroom 2
11'-8" x 14'-8"
Gameroom
13' x 15'
Bedroom 3
11' x 15'
Bath 2
Linen
Desk
Seat
Seat

WIDTH 59' 4"
DEPTH 44' 4"

DESIGN M9000
BEDROOMS 3
BATHROOMS 2½
FIRST FLOOR 1,669 Sq. Ft.
SECOND FLOOR 780 Sq. Ft.
TOTAL 2,449 Sq. Ft.
PRICE A5

This Farmhouse design will suit the needs of any large, active family. The foyer opens directly to the formal living room with an elegant fireplace. The family area offers a unique brick wall with built-in fireplace and a French door opening onto a covered porch. A well-planned kitchen overlooks a breakfast area with full-length windows that allow an uninterrupted view of the rear yard. The master bedroom, with third fireplace, has access to a private study. His and Hers walk-in closets, along with a garden tub and glass-enclosed shower, complete this secluded master suite. Upstairs, three bedrooms and two baths offer plenty of space and convenience for the children. A game room with an alcove provides a versatile family activity area.

9' Clg. Throughout

FIRST FLOOR

SECOND FLOOR

DESIGN	M9004
BEDROOMS	4
BATHROOMS	3½
FIRST FLOOR	2,166 Sq. Ft.
SECOND FLOOR	1,169 Sq. Ft.
TOTAL	3,335 Sq. Ft.
PRICE	A5

WIDTH 74' 8"
DEPTH 71' 8

FIRST FLOOR

10' Clg. Throughout First Floor
Unless Otherwise Noted

SECOND FLOOR

9' Clg. Throughout Second Floor
Unless Otherwise Noted

WIDTH 79'
DEPTH 60' 6"

The wraparound front porch and dormer windows give this home a casual and comfortable appearance. The large living area features French doors on each side of an elegant fireplace, and a built-in wet bar. An island cooktop, along with a walk-in pantry, are part of the well-planned kitchen. The utility room, with extra work space, leads to an attached two-car garage and storage area. The master bedroom has generous closet space and a two-way fireplace opening into the master bath. Bedrooms 3 and 4 each have a private bath, while bedroom 2 shares access to a bath with the game room. Each upstairs bedroom has a sloped ceiling and a cozy alcove created by the dormer window.

DESIGN	M9005
BEDROOMS	4
BATHROOMS	4
FIRST FLOOR	1,995 Sq. Ft.
SECOND FLOOR	1,077 Sq. Ft.
TOTAL	3,072 Sq. Ft.
PRICE	A5

VICTORIAN-STYLE FARMHOUSE

This home was inspired by the grand Farmhouses of the late 19th and early 20th Centuries, with their sprawling porches and Victorian-style gingerbread trim. The gallery leads from the elegant foyer to an enormous living and dining area. The spectacular kitchen opens directly to a windowed breakfast alcove and a light-filled sunroom, ideal for casual family living. Located off the kitchen is a walk-in pantry and a mudroom with additional storage. The first-floor master bedroom offers a secluded retreat. The bath area has His and Hers walk-in closets, a shower, and a garden tub with leaded-glass windows above. Upstairs, the two bedrooms each have private bathrooms and large walk-in closets. Includes plans for a detached two-car garage.

FIRST FLOOR

9' Clg. Throughout
Unless Otherwise Noted

DESIGN	M9075
BEDROOMS	3
BATHROOMS	3½
FIRST FLOOR	2,232 Sq. Ft.
SECOND FLOOR	808 Sq. Ft.
TOTAL	3,040 Sq. Ft.
PRICE	A5

WIDTH 75' 10"
DEPTH 46' 10"

SECOND FLOOR

9' Clg. Throughout First Floor

FIRST FLOOR

Util.
Breakfast
9' x 9'

Linen
Bath

Kitchen
12' x 13'

Dining
11' x 11'-4"

Up

Master Bedroom
15'-4" x 16'-4"

Living Room
15'-4" x 20'

Raised
Foyer

Porch

Wet Bar · Slope Clg.

Gameroom
14'-8" x 20'-8"
10' Clg.

Bedroom 4
11'-4" x 11'

Bath 3

Bath 2

Bedroom 2
13' x 16'-4"

Foyer
Below

Bedroom 3
11'-8" x 11'

Balcony

8' Clg. Throughout Second Floor
Unless Otherwise Noted

SECOND FLOOR

This Folk-Style Farmhouse is typical of those built in small communities in the south-central part of the United States around the turn of the century. Massive paneled columns and railing support the front porch. Inside, a raised foyer overlooks the living and dining areas. The kitchen features an island counter with sink and dish-washer. A spiral staircase provides convenient access to the second-floor game room, with ten-foot raised ceiling and wet bar. The first-floor master bedroom has two full-length windows for plenty of natural light, and a bath that features a glass-enclosed shower, garden tub, and mirrored doors at the walk-in closet. Plans for a detached two-car garage are included.

WIDTH 53' 4"
DEPTH 45' 4"

DESIGN M9076
BEDROOMS 4
BATHROOMS 3½
FIRST FLOOR 1,576 Sq. Ft.
SECOND FLOOR 1,242 Sq. Ft.
TOTAL 2,818 Sq. Ft.
PRICE A3

LARRY W. GARNETT & ASSOCIATES, INC.

Larry W. Garnett & Associates, Inc. offers a complete and useful plan package as outlined below:

- Elevations of front, rear and sides
- Foundation plan (monolithic concrete slab)
- Detailed floor plan(s) with electrical and plumbing locations
- Cabinet, vanity and miscellaneous interior details
- Typical detail and section sheets
- Garage plan (A two-car garage plan is included at no extra charge with all plans designed for a detached garage. See illustration below.)
- Reversed plans are mirror-image with dimensions and lettering reading backwards.

Plans do not include specifications or heating and air conditioning layouts. Your local mechanical contractor will size and locate the proper equipment for your particular climatic conditions. Material lists are not included due to differences in construction practices and local availability of various materials.

Larry W. Garnett & Associates, Inc. makes no warranties, either expressed or implied, regarding plans. Purchasers should have plans reviewed by a licensed builder and architect before beginning construction. Modification may be necessary for compliance with local and state regulations and codes.

BLUEPRINT PRICE SCHEDULE

	A1	A2	A3	A4	A5
One-set package	$185	$225	$250	$295	$325
Each additional set of same plan	$25				
Reversed set of same plan	$25				

	A6
One-set package	$425
Each additional set of same plan	$30
Reversed set of same plan	$30

2-Car Garage
23'-4" x 23'-4"

TO ORDER BLUEPRINTS, TURN TO PAGE 187.

For more information on these plans, write:
Larry W. Garnett & Associates, Inc., 4710 Vista Road, Pasadena, Texas 77505

HOME PLANNERS, INC.

"Modern Traditionalists," is how Charles W. Talcott, Chairman of Home Planners, Inc., describes the fifty-year-old company. "We give emphasis to detail and authenticity in our designs, remaining true to a style architecturally, while updating the floor plans to create a modern, comfortable home. This combination of classic architectural style and easy livability adds up to solid, long-lasting value."

Home Planners is one of the longest-running and most successful home design firms in the United States. With over 2,500 designs in its portfolio, the company provides a wide range of styles, sizes and types of homes. It takes pride in producing one of the most complete and detailed blueprint packages available and offers a number of additional products, including a home-planning kit, construction details sets and materials lists for most of its designs.

With over 135 books and magazines to its credit, Home Planners has sold over 2½ million sets of blueprints since its inception in 1946. The company's plans are featured regularly in such popular magazines as *House Beautiful, Better Homes and Gardens, Practical Homeowner, Homeowner, Decorating/Remodeling* and others. Among the many books published by Home Planners are collections of exterior styles, design categories and portfolios. In addition to the plans, many of the publications provide special sections offering advice, building and design tips and helpful hints. Of particular note is *The Home Landscaper,* a bestselling guide to landscape design with 40 professionally designed plans the homeowner can create from blueprints.

Home Planners' portfolio of Victorian and Farmhouse designs is a response to a growing demand for these styles. Rickard Bailey, President and Publisher of Home Planners, maintains, "Today, there is a return to traditionalism and pure styles. People want the look and feel of an older home with the amenities and comforts of modern floor planning. Elaborate master bedroom suites, cozy country kitchens, libraries, media centers and great rooms are all a part of what makes a plan livable.

"Featured here are Victorian and Farmhouse designs created to meet the needs of today's sophisticated family. Ranging in size from 1,515 to 5,643 square feet, these plans represent some of the best examples of the genre. Included are 18 brand new, never-before-published plans, many with smaller square footages and all boasting features that enhance their appeal."

The featured Victorians are presented with all the architectural details that make this style so unique: sweeping wraparound verandas, Palladian windows, cornice adornments, spindlework and much more. Inside, they boast such sought-after amenities as pampering master bedroom suites, third-floor guest suites, studies, libraries, media rooms and exercise rooms.

The Farmhouses are a countrified collection of one- and two-story homes with rustic exterior detailing and interiors that have all the components of modern floor planning: gathering rooms, split-bedroom layouts, country kitchens and convenient service areas, as well as other contemporary comforts.

Concludes Bailey: "All of these plans have been created with the care and professional expertise that fifty years of experience in the home-planning business affords us. Though clearly visually appealing and true to their architectural past, these homes are designed to be built, lived in and enjoyed today and for years to come."

This delightful Victorian cottage features three floors of living potential and exterior details that perfectly complement the convenient plan inside. Note the central placement of the kitchen, near to the dining room and the family room. A lovely side porch is the ideal location for weekend relaxing. Two fireplaces keep things warm and cozy. Three second-floor bedrooms include a master suite with bay window and two family bedrooms, one with an alcove and walk-in closet. Use the third-floor studio as a study, office or playroom for the children.

FIRST FLOOR

SECOND FLOOR

WIDTH 48'
DEPTH 46'

THIRD FLOOR

DESIGN	M3383
BEDROOMS	3
BATHROOMS	2½
FIRST FLOOR	995 Sq. Ft.
SECOND FLOOR	1,064 Sq. Ft.
THIRD FLOOR	425 Sq. Ft.
TOTAL	2,484 Sq. Ft.
PRICE	B3

FIRST FLOOR

WIDTH 38'
DEPTH 52'

SECOND FLOOR

ATTIC

Victorian houses are well known for their orientation on narrow building sites. Even when this occurs, none of the captivating exterior styling is lost. This house is but 38-feet wide. Its narrow width belies the tremendous amount of livability found inside. And, of course, the ubiquitous porch/veranda contributes mightily to style as well as livability. The efficient, U-shaped kitchen is flanked by the informal breakfast room and formal dining room. The rear living area is spacious and functions in an exciting manner with the outdoor areas. Upstairs, the master bedroom features a deluxe bath with a walk-in closet, separate tub and shower, and a double vanity. Two additional bedrooms have extra large closets. Bonus recreational, hobby and storage space is offered in the basement and the attic.

DESIGN	M2974
BEDROOMS	3
BATHROOMS	2½
FIRST FLOOR	911 Sq. Ft.
SECOND FLOOR	861 Sq. Ft.
TOTAL	1,772 Sq. Ft.
PRICE	B1

Covered porches front and rear are the first signal that this is a fine example of Folk Victorian styling. Complementing the exterior is a grand plan for family living. A formal living room and attached dining room provide space for entertaining guests. The large family room with fireplace is a gathering room for everyday. Both areas have access to outdoor spaces. Four bedrooms occupy the second floor. The master suite features two lavatories, a window seat and three closets. One of the family bedrooms has its own private balcony and could be used as a study. Note the open staircase and convenient linen storage.

FIRST FLOOR

SECOND FLOOR

DESIGN M3385
BEDROOMS 3 or 4 (study)
BATHROOMS 2½
FIRST FLOOR 1,096 Sq. Ft.
SECOND FLOOR 900 Sq. Ft.
TOTAL 1,996 Sq. Ft.
PRICE B3

WIDTH 56'
DEPTH 44'

FIRST FLOOR

SECOND FLOOR

This two-story farmhouse will be a delight for those who spend much time working at home. The second floor offers the utmost in privacy, with a secluded master bedroom full of comforting features and a studio for more industrious pursuits. Downstairs is a very livable floor plan. A U-shaped kitchen with snack bar and breakfast area with bay window and desk are only the first of the eating areas, which extend to a formal dining room and a covered rear porch for dining al fresco. The two-story living room features a cozy fireplace. A versatile room to the back could serve as a media room or a third bedroom, sharing a full bath with the large front bedroom with bay window.

DESIGN	M3390
BEDROOMS	2 or 3
BATHROOMS	2
FIRST FLOOR	1,472 Sq. Ft.
SECOND FLOOR	1,116 Sq. Ft.
TOTAL	2,588 Sq. Ft.
PRICE	B3

WIDTH 52'
DEPTH 58' 6"

A stunning Victorian turret accents the facade of this compact three-story beauty, a promise of the exciting floor plan held inside. Downstairs rooms include a grand-sized living room/ dining room combination that handles both formal and informal gatherings. The U-shaped kitchen has a snack-bar pass-through to the dining room. Just to the left of the entry foyer is a private study with wet bar. On the second floor are three bedrooms and two full baths. The master bedroom has a whirlpool spa and large walk-in closet. The third floor is a perfect location for a guest bedroom with private bath, dormer window and two closets. Be sure to notice the full-width covered porch stretching across the back of the house.

DESIGN M3389
BEDROOMS 4
BATHROOMS 3½
FIRST FLOOR 1,161 Sq. Ft.
SECOND FLOOR 1,090 Sq. Ft.
THIRD FLOOR 488 Sq. Ft.
TOTAL 2,739 Sq. Ft.
PRICE B3

WIDTH 40' 4"
DEPTH 68' 6"

Detailing is one of the characteristic features of Queen Anne Victorians and this home has no lack of it: spindlework, pediment ornamentation, fish-scale shingles and a lovely oval-shaped window. Interior rooms add just the right living patterns. Special features include a powder room for guests in the front hallway, a through-fireplace between the ample gathering room and cozy study, an efficient U-shaped kitchen with pantry, and a full-width terrace to the rear. On the second floor are three bedrooms—one a master suite with walk-in closet and amenity-filled bath. An open balcony overlooks the gathering room.

FIRST FLOOR

TERRACE

GATHERING RM
14⁴ X 17⁰

STUDY
11⁸ X 14⁴

DINING RM
11⁰ X 10⁰

OPEN THRU

BALCONY ABOVE

KITCHEN
13⁰ X 10⁰

LAUNDRY

PDR RM

FOYER

BRKFST RM
11⁰ X 8⁸

COVERED PORCH

GARAGE
22⁴ X 22⁰ · STORAGE

STORAGE

SECOND FLOOR

GATHERING RM BELOW

SLOPED CEILING

BEDROOM
11⁰ X 10⁴

MASTER BEDROOM
11⁸ X 16⁰

BALCONY

LINEN

BATH

WALK-IN CLOSET

MASTER BATH

WHIRLPOOL

VANITY

FOYER BELOW

BEDROOM
11⁰ X 10⁴

SLOPED CEILING

ATTIC

ROOF DECK

WIDTH 47'
DEPTH 58' 4"

DESIGN	M3391
BEDROOMS	3
BATHROOMS	2½
FIRST FLOOR	1,230 Sq. Ft.
SECOND FLOOR	991 Sq. Ft.
TOTAL	2,221 Sq. Ft.
PRICE	B3

A turreted facade, dormer window and fish-scale shingle details make this moderately sized Victorian stand out at a glance. Its well-designed floor plans make it even more attractive. Notice how guests as well as family are accommodated: powder room in the front foyer; gathering room with terrace access, fireplace and attached formal dining room; split-bedroom sleeping arrangements. The master suite contains His and Hers walk-in closets, a separate shower and whirlpool tub and a delightful bay-windowed area. Upstairs there are three more bedrooms (one could serve as a study, one as a media room), a full bath and an open lounge area overlooking the gathering room. Notice the covered porches front and rear and long terrace area.

DESIGN	M3393
BEDROOMS	3 or 4 (study or media room)
BATHROOMS	2½
FIRST FLOOR	1,449 Sq. Ft.
SECOND FLOOR	902 Sq. Ft.
TOTAL	2,351 Sq. Ft.
PRICE	B3

FIRST FLOOR

SECOND FLOOR

WIDTH 49'
DEPTH 54' 4"

FIRST FLOOR

COVERED PORCH

FAMILY KITCHEN
21⁸ x 15⁴ +BAY

LIBRARY
12¹⁰ x 11⁸

RANGE

WASH RM

MUD RM

LAUNDRY

HALL

FOYER

DINING RM
10⁸ x 12⁰

CURB

LIVING RM
12¹⁰ x 20¹⁰

COVERED PORCH

GARAGE
21² x 23⁸

UP

SECOND FLOOR

WHIRLPOOL

BEDROOM
12⁶ x 12⁸

WALK-IN CLOSET

SEAT

M. BATH

VANITY

BATH

WALK-IN CLOSET

LIN

RAILING

DN

ROOF

UPPER FOYER

BEDROOM
10⁸ x 13⁰

MASTER BEDROOM
12¹⁰ x 20¹⁰

WIDTH 57' 6"
DEPTH 46'

Classic Victorian styling comes to the forefront in this Queen Anne two-story. Complementary fishscale-adorned pediments top the bayed tower to the left and garage to the right. Smaller versions are found at the dormer windows above a spindle-work porch. The interior boasts comfortable living quarters for the entire family. On opposite sides of the wide foyer are the formal dining and living rooms. To the rear is a country-style island kitchen with attached family room (don't miss the fireplace here). A small library shares a covered porch with this informal gathering area and also has its own fireplace. Three bedrooms on the second floor include a master suite with grand bath. The two family bathrooms share a full bath. Take special note of the service area conveniently attached to the two-car garage.

DESIGN	M3384
BEDROOMS	3
BATHROOMS	2½
FIRST FLOOR	1,399 Sq. Ft.
SECOND FLOOR	1,123 Sq. Ft.
TOTAL	2,522 Sq. Ft.
PRICE	B3

A simple but charming Queen Anne Victorian, this enchanting three-story home is our featured cover design. The exterior boasts delicately turned rails and decorated columns on its covered front porch. Just above is a small covered balcony off the master bedroom on the second floor. Inside is a family-oriented floor plan that includes a living room with fireplace and dining room that connects to the gourmet family kitchen via a wet bar. The adjoining family room contains another fireplace with a raised hearth complemented by flanking windows. The second floor holds two bedrooms, one a master suite with grand bath. A tucked-away guest suite on the third floor has its own private bath. Notice the unique gazebo projection off the covered porch to the rear of the plan.

DESIGN	M3382
BEDROOMS	3
BATHROOMS	3½
FIRST FLOOR	1,366 Sq. Ft.
SECOND FLOOR	837 Sq. Ft.
THIRD FLOOR	363 Sq. Ft.
TOTAL	2,566 Sq. Ft.
PRICE	B3

FIRST FLOOR

SECOND FLOOR

THIRD FLOOR

WIDTH 50' 2"
DEPTH 69' 3"

RIGHT SIDE ELEVATION

REAR ELEVATION

QUEEN ANNE

One of the most popular features of the Victorian house has always been its covered porches. These finely detailed outdoor living spaces may be found on the front, the side, the rear or even all three locations at once. This design shows just that. In addition to being an appealing design feature, covered porches have their practical side, too. They provide wonderful indoor/outdoor living relationships. Imagine sheltered outdoor living facilities for the various formal and informal living and dining areas of the plan. This home has a myriad of features to cater to the living requirements of the growing, active family. The modern kitchen features a snack bar and a desk. The luxurious master bath with His and Hers walk-in closets, a whirlpool tub and a double vanity will be greatly appreciated. Notice the built-in shelves in the bayed front bedroom.

DESIGN	M2973
BEDROOMS	4
BATHROOMS	2½
FIRST FLOOR	1,269 Sq. Ft.
SECOND FLOOR	1,227 Sq. Ft.
TOTAL	2,496 Sq. Ft.
PRICE	B2

FIRST FLOOR

WIDTH 70'
DEPTH 44' 4"

SECOND FLOOR

FIRST FLOOR

VERANDA

RAILING

ROOF ABOVE

FAMILY RM
21⁰x13⁴

BREAKFAST RM
14⁰x11⁴

KITCHEN
10⁰x11⁴

DINING RM
13⁰x11⁴+BAY

PASS THRU

DESK

PANTRY

REFG

BC

PDR RM

LAUNDRY
10⁰x7⁴

PANTRY

D W LT CL

CL

CURB

UP

LIVING RM
16⁸x13⁴

VERANDA

UP

RAILING

GARAGE
21⁴x21⁸+STORAGE

STORAGE

BEDROOM
11⁰x13⁰

SEAT

BATH

MASTER BEDROOM
13⁰x13⁰

WHIRLPOOL

BATH

WALK-IN CLOSET

CL

DN

LIN

CL

STUDY
9⁰x14⁰

BEDROOM
13⁰x10⁴

UP

SECOND FLOOR

WIDTH 62' 7"
DEPTH 54'

Covered porches in the front and back are a fine preview to the livable nature of this Victorian. The expansive sunken family room features a fireplace and access to the out-of-doors. This plan includes both a formal dining room with a bay and a living room as well as a breakfast room. The kitchen features a pass-through and a large pantry. A second pantry, as well as a closet, are placed conveniently near the garage entrance. An ample laundry room, garage with storage area, and powder room round out the first floor. The master bedroom features an elegant bath with a whirlpool tub, a separate shower with a seat, and a double vanity. Plenty of storage is available in two closets. The second floor also contains two additional bedrooms, a study and a bath.

DESIGN	M3309
BEDROOMS	3
BATHROOMS	2½
FIRST FLOOR	1,375 Sq. Ft.
SECOND FLOOR	1,016 Sq. Ft.
TOTAL	2,391 Sq. Ft.
PRICE	B2

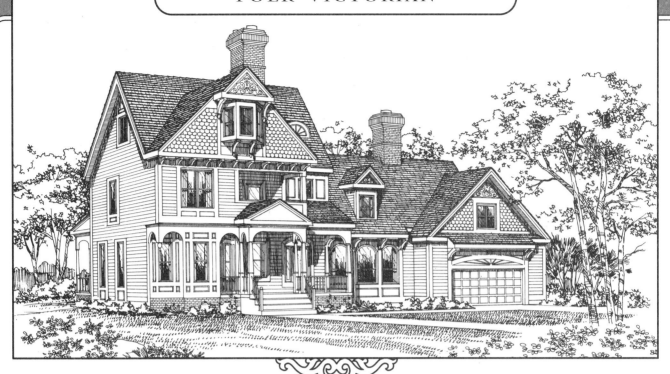

Though somewhat less elaborate than other Victorian types, the Folk Victorian is nevertheless an important and delightful interpretation as evidenced by this three-story example. From lovely covered front porch to classic rear veranda, it offers the finest in modern floor plans. The formal living areas are set off by a family room which connects the main house to the service areas. The laundry has room for not only a washer and dryer but also a freezer and sewing area. The second floor holds three bedrooms and two full baths. A sitting area in the master suite separates it from family bedrooms. On the third floor is a guest bedroom with gracious bath and large walk-in closet. Note the large storage area in the third-floor hall.

FIRST FLOOR

SECOND FLOOR

THIRD FLOOR

WIDTH 70'
DEPTH 40'

DESIGN	M3394
BEDROOMS	4
BATHROOMS	3½
FIRST FLOOR	1,531 Sq. Ft.
SECOND FLOOR	1,307 Sq. Ft.
THIRD FLOOR	664 Sq. Ft.
TOTAL	3,502 Sq. Ft.
PRICE	B4

FIRST FLOOR

STORAGE
10⁸ x ..

WASH RM

LAUND

MUD RM

FAMILY RM
13¹⁰ x 19⁰

BRKFAST
10⁶ x 13⁴

KITCHEN
10⁰ x 13⁴

COOK TOP

DINING RM
11⁰ x 13⁴ + BAY

PANTRY

OVENS

BC

PDR RM

FOYER

UP

DN

GARAGE
22⁸ x 23⁸ + BAY

CURB

COVERED PORCH

COVERED PORCH

LIVING RM
15² x 19⁴ + BAY

UP

DN

SECOND FLOOR

WINDOW WELL

BEDROOM
16⁴ x 13⁴

WHIRLPOOL

M. BATH

SEAT

ROOF

VANITY

BEDROOM
13⁸ x 14⁸

HER WALK-IN CLOSET

HIS WALK-IN CLOSET

RAILING

OPEN

DESK

CL

BATH

DN

UP

ROOF

SEAT

LINEN

MASTER BEDROOM
15² x 15⁰ + BAY

WINDOW WELL

THIRD FLOOR

ROOF

LIN

LIN

BATH

RAILING

S

GUEST BEDROOM
12⁸ x 13⁴

CL

DN

WINDOW WELL

ROOF

ATTIC

WIDTH 70'
DEPTH 44'

A testament to real Folk Victorian styling, this delightful home offers the best in thoughtful floor planning. From the covered front porch the home opens to a well-executed entry foyer. To the left is the casual family room with fireplace and proximity to the laundry and mud rooms. To the right is the formal living room with bay window and fireplace. This room connects to the formal dining area, also with bay window. The kitchen/breakfast room combination features sliding glass doors to the rear covered porch, an island cook top and large pantry. Second-floor bedrooms include a well-planned master suite and two family bedrooms served by a full bath. A guest room dominates the third floor and features its own private bath.

DESIGN M3388
BEDROOMS 4
BATHROOMS 3½+powder rm
FIRST FLOOR 1,517 Sq. Ft.
SECOND FLOOR 1,267 Sq. Ft.
THIRD FLOOR 480 Sq. Ft.
TOTAL 3,264 Sq. Ft.
PRICE B4

The spacious foyer of this Victorian welcomes you to a practical and efficient interior. The formal living and dining area is located to one side of the plan. Both rooms function well together and have access to the covered veranda. Spaciousness is the byword with a glorious two-story sloping ceiling and open planning between the two rooms. The more active area of the plan includes the fine U-shaped kitchen which opens to the family room. Double French doors provide access to the veranda from the family room while the kitchen looks out upon it. The library with built-in shelves and access to the front yard will offer a full measure of privacy. Upstairs, the master bedroom with fireplace is joined by two other bedrooms.

FIRST FLOOR

SECOND FLOOR

WIDTH 64'
DEPTH 49' 4"

DESIGN	M2972
BEDROOMS	3
BATHROOMS	2½
FIRST FLOOR	1,432 Sq. Ft.
SECOND FLOOR	1,108 Sq. Ft.
TOTAL	2,540 Sq. Ft.
PRICE	B2

FIRST FLOOR

SECOND FLOOR

WIDTH 64'
DEPTH 51' 8"

Classically styled, this charming design brings together the best in historical styling and modern floor planning. Special exterior features include three verandas, multi-paned windows and arch-topped windows. Inside, the first-floor plan boasts formal living and dining areas on either side of the entry foyer, a study that could double as a guest room with nearby full bath, a large family room with raised-hearth fireplace and snack bar pass-through, and a U-shaped kitchen with attached break-fast room. Two family bedrooms on the second floor share a full bath; the master bedroom has a thoughtfully appointed bath and large walk-in closet.

DESIGN	M3307
BEDROOMS	3 or 4 (study)
BATHROOMS	3
FIRST FLOOR	1,765 Sq. Ft.
SECOND FLOOR	1,105 Sq. Ft.
TOTAL	2,870 Sq. Ft.
PRICE	B3

The stately proportions and exquisite Victorian detailing of this home are exciting indeed. Like so many Victorian houses, interesting roof lines set the character of this design. Observe the delightful mixture of gable roof, hip roof and dramatic turret. Horizontal siding, wood shingling, wide fascia, rake and corner boards make a strong statement. The delicate detailing of the windows, railings, cornices and front entry is most appealing to the eye. Inside is a very livable plan. The kitchen features a center island cooktop and shares a wide counter for casual dining with the adjoining family room. A bayed dining room with access to the rear porch is available for more formal occasions. Upstairs, each of the four bedrooms features a bay area and plenty of closet space. Don't miss the spacious master bath.

FIRST FLOOR

DESIGN	M2971
BEDROOMS	4
BATHROOMS	2½
FIRST FLOOR	1,766 Sq. Ft.
SECOND FLOOR	1,519 Sq. Ft.
TOTAL	3,285 Sq. Ft.
PRICE	B3

LEFT SIDE ELEVATION

WIDTH 77' 6"
DEPTH 44' 4"

SECOND FLOOR

What can beat the charm of a turreted Victorian with covered porches to the front, side and rear? Projecting bays make their contribution to exterior styling and provide an extra measure of livability to the living, dining and family rooms, plus two of the bedrooms. The efficient kitchen, with its island cooking station, functions well with the dining and family rooms. A study provides a quiet first-floor haven for the family's less active pursuits. Upstairs, there are three big bedrooms and a fine master bath. A third floor provides a guest suite and huge bulk storage area (make it a cedar closet if you wish). This house has a basement for the development of further recreational and storage facilities. Note the two fireplaces, large laundry and attached two-car garage.

DESIGN	M2969
BEDROOMS	4
BATHROOMS	3½
FIRST FLOOR	1,618 Sq. Ft.
SECOND FLOOR	1,315 Sq. Ft.
THIRD FLOOR	477 Sq. Ft.
TOTAL	3,410 Sq. Ft.
PRICE	B3

FIRST FLOOR

THIRD FLOOR

WIDTH 71' 8"
DEPTH 48' 4"

SECOND FLOOR

FIRST FLOOR

Reminiscent of the Gothic Victorian style of the mid-19th Century, this delightfully detailed, three-story house has a wraparound veranda for summertime relaxing. A grand reception hall welcomes visitors and displays an elegant staircase. The parlor and family room, each with a fireplace, provide excellent formal and informal living facilities. The well-planned kitchen is only a couple of steps from the dining and breakfast rooms. Access to the rear terrace is provided through the family room or the breakfast room. The second floor has four bedrooms and two baths plus a sewing room or study. The third floor houses an additional bedroom or studio with a half bath, as well as a playroom.

SECOND FLOOR

THIRD FLOOR

WIDTH 88'
DEPTH 42'

DESIGN	M2645
BEDROOMS	4
BATHROOMS	2½+powder rm
FIRST FLOOR	1,600 Sq. Ft.
SECOND FLOOR	1,305 Sq. Ft.
THIRD FLOOR	925 Sq. Ft.
TOTAL	3,830 Sq. Ft.
PRICE	B3

This home is a lovely example of classic Queen Anne architecture with two turrets, and pediments over the entry and three dormer-style window areas. Its floor plan offers over 5,000 square feet of living potential in three floors. On the first floor are the activity areas: a gathering room with fireplace, a study with an octagonal window area, a formal dining room and a kitchen with attached breakfast room. Bedrooms on the second floor include three family bedrooms and a grand master suite with sitting area, dressing room and master bath. A large attic storage area is found over the garage. On the third floor are a guest room with private bath and sitting area, and a game room with attached library.

FIRST FLOOR

SECOND FLOOR

THIRD FLOOR

DESIGN	M3395
BEDROOMS	5
BATHROOMS	3½
FIRST FLOOR	2,248 Sq. Ft.
SECOND FLOOR	2,020 Sq. Ft.
THIRD FLOOR	1,117 Sq. Ft.
TOTAL	5,385 Sq. Ft.
PRICE	B5

WIDTH 92'
DEPTH 53' 4"

SECOND FLOOR

THIRD FLOOR

FIRST FLOOR

WIDTH 64'
DEPTH 67'

This beautiful Folk Victorian has all the properties of others in its class but measures them out in proportions that make it seem estate-like. The interior amenities are found on a corresponding scale as well. Living areas include a formal Victorian parlor, a private study and large gathering room. The formal dining room has its more casual counterpart in a bay-windowed breakfast room. Both are near the well-appointed kitchen. Five bedrooms serve family and guest needs handily. Three bedrooms on the second floor include a luxurious master suite. For outdoor entertaining or simply weekend relaxing, there is a covered rear porch leading to a terrace.

DESIGN	M3386
BEDROOMS	5
BATHROOMS	3½
FIRST FLOOR	1,683 Sq. Ft.
SECOND FLOOR	1,388 Sq. Ft.
THIRD FLOOR	808 Sq. Ft.
TOTAL	3,879 Sq. Ft.
PRICE	B5

Named for the architect, Henry Hobson Richardson, the Richardson Romanesque is known for being ample in size and substantial in appearance. This three-story example is indicative of the style's best characteristics. Complementary arched turrets on the outside give way to a wonderfully convenient floor plan. Formal and informal living areas occupy the first floor in a living room, dining room, family room and grand country kitchen. Upstairs are two family bedrooms and a lavish master suite with sitting area. The third floor contains another bedroom and private bath that could serve guests or live-ins quite well. Full-width verandas, front and back, provide indoor/outdoor living relationships and add just the right Victorian touch.

FIRST FLOOR

SECOND FLOOR

THIRD FLOOR

DESIGN	M3392
BEDROOMS	4
BATHROOMS	3½
FIRST FLOOR	1,405 Sq. Ft.
SECOND FLOOR	1,430 Sq. Ft.
THIRD FLOOR	624 Sq. Ft.
TOTAL	3,459 Sq. Ft.
PRICE	B4

WIDTH 62' 4"
DEPTH 51' 4"

FIRST FLOOR

SECOND FLOOR

THIRD FLOOR

WIDTH 100'
DEPTH 48'

Another design that borrows from the forceful style of Henry Hobson Richardson, this home features a rounded turret top and rounded arches on the turret's windows. The interior allows plenty of room for busy lifestyles. Besides formal living and dining rooms and a casual family gathering room, there is a study with corner fireplace that also serves as a media room. Three bedrooms are found on the second floor along with two full baths. The third floor contains another bedroom with full bath and small alcove. Wide verandas both front and rear and a screened porch just off the family room allow good indoor/outdoor living relationships. Notice the large hobby/laundry area connecting the house to the garage.

DESIGN M3387
BEDROOMS 4
BATHROOMS 3½+powder rm
FIRST FLOOR 2,393 Sq. Ft.
SECOND FLOOR 1,703 Sq. Ft.
THIRD FLOOR 716 Sq. Ft.
TOTAL 4,812 Sq. Ft.
PRICE B5

A porch, is a porch, is a porch. But, when it wraps around to a side, or even two sides of the house, we call it a veranda. This charming Victorian features a covered outdoor living area on all four sides! It even ends as a screened porch with a sun deck above. This interesting plan offers three floors of livability. And what livability it is! Fireplaces can be found in the living room, family room and master suite. Plenty of formal and informal living facilities to go along with the potential of five bedrooms. The master suite is just that—a full suite. It is adjacent to an interesting sitting room and sports a sun deck and excellent bath/personal care facilities. The third floor will make a wonderful haven for the family's student members.

FIRST FLOOR

DESIGN	M2970
BEDROOMS	5
BATHROOMS	3½
FIRST FLOOR	1,538 Sq. Ft.
SECOND FLOOR	1,526 Sq. Ft.
THIRD FLOOR	658 Sq. Ft.
TOTAL	3,722 Sq. Ft.
PRICE	B4

WIDTH 67'
DEPTH 66'

LEFT SIDE ELEVATION

SECOND FLOOR

THIRD FLOOR

QUEEN ANNE

Victorian Style is displayed in exqui-site proportions in this three-bed-room, four-bath home. From veran-das, both front and rear, to the stately turrets and impressive chimney stack, this home is a beauty. Inside is a superb floor plan with many thought-ful amenities. The large living room and two-story family room both have fireplaces. To the front, there is a cozy study for private time. A gour-met kitchen with built-ins has a pass-through counter to the breakfast room. The bayed formal dining room has access to both the front and rear verandas. The master suite on the second floor includes many special features: whirlpool spa, separate shower, His and Hers walk-in closets, a private vanity, large exercise room, and a fireplace. There are two more bedrooms, each with a full bath, on the second floor.

FIRST FLOOR

SECOND FLOOR

DESIGN	M3304
BEDROOMS	3
BATHROOMS	4
FIRST FLOOR	2,102 Sq. Ft.
SECOND FLOOR	1,971 Sq. Ft.
TOTAL	4,073 Sq. Ft.
PRICE	B5

WIDTH 87'
DEPTH 58' 6"

FIRST FLOOR

SECOND FLOOR

Uniquely shaped rooms and a cache of amenities highlight this three-story beauty. The large sunken family room features a fireplace, wet bar and built-in seat. A liberal amount of work space is available in the kitchen, the breakfast room with built-in desk, and the laundry. Notice the abundance of storage space and the butler's pantry. A four-car garage easily holds the family fleet. The second floor has two family bedrooms and a full bath plus a master suite with His and Hers closets, multiple vanities and a whirlpool bath. An exercise room on the third floor has its own sauna and bath, while the large guest room on this floor is complemented by a charming alcove and another full bath.

THIRD FLOOR

WIDTH 90' 6"
DEPTH 60'

DESIGN	M3308
BEDROOMS	4
BATHROOMS	3½+powder rm
FIRST FLOOR	2,515 Sq. Ft.
SECOND FLOOR	1,708 Sq. Ft.
THIRD FLOOR	1,001 Sq. Ft.
TOTAL	5,224 Sq. Ft.
PRICE	B5

This enchanting manor displays architectural elements typical of the Victorian Style: asymmetrical facade, decorative shingles and gables, and a covered porch. The two-story living room with fireplace and wet bar opens to the glass-enclosed rear porch with skylights. A spacious kitchen is filled with amenities, including a butler's pantry connecting to the dining room. The master suite, adjacent to the study, opens to the rear deck. A cozy fireplace keeps the room warm on chilly evenings. The second floor opens to a large lounge with built-in cabinets and bookshelves. Three bedrooms and two full baths complete the second-floor livability. The three-car garage contains disappearing stairs to an attic storage area.

FIRST FLOOR

WIDTH 118' 4"
DEPTH 54' 6"

SECOND FLOOR

DESIGN M2954
BEDROOMS 4
BATHROOMS 3½+powder rm
FIRST FLOOR 3,079 Sq. Ft.
SECOND FLOOR 1,461 Sq. Ft.
TOTAL 4,540 Sq. Ft.
PRICE B5

SECOND FLOOR

FIRST FLOOR

LOUNGE 15⁰ x 16⁰

BEDROOM 18⁶ x 12⁰

UPPER GREAT RM

WALK-IN CLOSET

BATH

BEDROOM 12⁸ x 14⁴

BATH

WALK-IN CLOSET

WALK-IN CLOSET

BATH

COMPUTER ALCOVE

BEDROOM 12⁰ x 12⁸

UPPER FOYER

BEDROOM 13⁰ x 18⁰

TERRACE

GARAGE 23⁴ x 36⁰

COVERED PORCH

MASTER BEDROOM 15⁰ x 20⁰

GREAT RM 23⁴ x 17⁴

W.R.

LAUNDRY 9⁶ x 8⁴

MORNING RM 12⁰ x 12⁰

BATH

SEAT

SEAT

WHIRLPOOL

DRESSING RM

OPEN ABOVE

COVERED PORCH

HER WALK-IN CLOSET

BOOK SHELVES

SITTING RM 15⁰ x 10⁸

PDR RM

OPEN ABOVE

KITCHEN 14⁰ x 16⁶

BUTLERS PANTRY

PANTRY

COVERED PORCH

BOOK SHELVES

LIBRARY 12⁰ x 17⁰

FOYER

DINING RM 13⁰ x 16⁰

COVERED PORCH

RAILING

A magnificent, finely wrought covered porch wraps around this impressive Victorian estate home. The gracious two-story foyer provides a direct view into the great room. To the left of the foyer is a bookshelf-lined library and to the right is a dramatic, octagonal-shaped dining room. The island cooktop completes a convenient work triangle in the kitchen, and a pass-through connects this room with the Victorian-style morning room. A luxurious master suite is located on the first floor and opens to the rear covered porch. A through-fireplace warms the bedroom, sitting room and dressing room, which includes His and Hers walk-in closets. Four uniquely designed bedrooms, three full baths, and a restful lounge with fireplace are located on the second floor.

DESIGN M2953
BEDROOMS 5
BATHROOMS 4 ½+powder rm
FIRST FLOOR 2,991 Sq. Ft.
SECOND FLOOR 1,802 Sq. Ft.
TOTAL 4,793 Sq. Ft.
PRICE B5

WIDTH 88'
DEPTH 91'

Signature Series — Luxury Homes

What a stylish departure from today's usual architecture. This refreshing exterior may be referred to as Neo-Victorian. Its vertical lines, steep roofs and variety of gables remind one of the old Gothic Victorian houses of yesteryear. This adaptation, without the decorative trimwork, has a distinctive appeal all its own. Notice the unique balcony over the covered porch of the front entrance. Inside, there is an efficiently working floor plan that is delightfully spacious. Not only do the informal family room and formal living room have fireplaces, but so does the sizable dining room. Notice the efficient kitchen, snack bar, laundry and handy powder room. Upstairs there are four large bedrooms and two full baths. Three of the bedrooms contain sloping ceilings, while the fourth contains a sunlit bay area.

FIRST FLOOR

SECOND FLOOR

DESIGN	M2646
BEDROOMS	4
BATHROOMS	2½
FIRST FLOOR	1,274 Sq. Ft.
SECOND FLOOR	1,322 Sq. Ft.
TOTAL	2,596 Sq. Ft.
PRICE	B2

WIDTH 65'
DEPTH 53'

SECOND FLOOR

BED RM
13⁴ x 11⁸

BED RM
11⁸ x 13⁰

SLOPED CEILING

SLOPED CEILING

CL

LINEN

BATH

OPEN TO LIVING ROOM BELOW

BALCONY

DN

OPEN

RAILING

BATH

CL

LINEN

CL

SLOPED CEILING

SLOPED CEILING

BED RM
13⁴ x 14⁰

BED RM
11⁸ x 11⁰

ROOF

FIRST FLOOR

TERRACE

DINING RM
15⁶ x 12⁰

NOOK
9⁶ x 11⁶

DN

FAMILY RM
21⁹ x 13⁰

RAISED HEARTH

OPEN THRU FIREPLACE

RANGE

KITCHEN
12⁰ x 10⁰

13⁰ CEILING

RAISED HEARTH

RAISED HEARTH

B.C.

SNACK BAR

8⁸ HIGH CABINET OPEN OVER

SHELVES

REF'G.

CAB'T.

CL

CL

B.C.

CAB'T.

UP

8" CURB

TERRACE

LIVING RM
20⁰ x 20⁰

OPEN ABOVE

DN

ENTRY

PDR. RM.

PORCH

GARAGE
23⁴ x 23⁴

WALK-IN CLOSET

MASTER BEDROOM
13⁸ x 16⁴ + BAY

BATH

WIDTH 78' 8"
DEPTH 54'

Another Neo-Victorian, and what an impressive and unique design it is. Observe the roof lines, the window treatment, the use of contrasting exterior materials and the arched, covered front entrance. The interior is equally breathtaking with spaciousness as the byword. Note that the entry and family room are two steps above the remainder of the first floor. The inside kitchen effectively functions with the dining room, nook and family room. The living room has a two-story ceiling and looks up at the second-floor balcony. A raised-hearth, through-fireplace serves both the living and dining rooms. A second fireplace is found in the family room. The master bedroom is conveniently located on the first floor, while upstairs there are four bedrooms and two baths for the younger generation.

DESIGN	M2647
BEDROOMS	5
BATHROOMS	3½
FIRST FLOOR	2,104 Sq. Ft.
SECOND FLOOR	1,230 Sq. Ft.
TOTAL	3,334 Sq. Ft.
PRICE	B4

This Neo-Victorian design with its many gables offers plenty of roomy comfort. The first floor includes a living room with fireplace and bay window, family room with fireplace, formal dining room, modern kitchen with snack bar and breakfast room, as well as a large foyer with a convenient powder room. Note the second staircase in the utility room. The second floor includes a master bedroom suite with three closets, a dressing room and a separate tub and shower; three other large bedrooms; and a large studio that could also double as a room for hobbies or storage. The third floor includes a guest bedroom with bath and an upper lounge.

FIRST FLOOR

THIRD FLOOR

SECOND FLOOR

DESIGN	M2874
BEDROOMS	5
BATHROOMS	3½+powder rm
FIRST FLOOR	1,661 Sq. Ft.
SECOND FLOOR	1,808 Sq. Ft.
THIRD FLOOR	436 Sq. Ft.
TOTAL	3,905 Sq. Ft.
PRICE	B4

WIDTH 66'
DEPTH 36'

NEO-VICTORIAN

FIRST FLOOR

SECOND FLOOR

WIDTH 81'
DEPTH 52' 8"

Detailed with gingerbread woodwork and a handsome double-width chimney, this two-story Neo-Victorian is breathtaking. Enter this home by way of the large, tiled receiving hall. The formal living room is spacious, with a fireplace and access to the covered porch. The dining room has a delightful bay window and is convenient to the kitchen for entertaining. The library is tucked between these two formal areas. The informal family room, with its L-shaped snack bar, will be a great place for family activities. Exploring the second floor reveals two bedrooms with two full bathrooms, and a third family bedroom nearby. The gracious master suite features His and Hers baths and a host of other features.

DESIGN	M2829
BEDROOMS	5
BATHROOMS	4
FIRST FLOOR	2,044 Sq. Ft.
SECOND FLOOR	1,962 Sq. Ft.
TOTAL	4,006 Sq. Ft.
PRICE	B4

This modest-sized Ranch House has much to offer in the way of livability. It may function as either a two- or three-bedroom home. The living room is huge and features a fine, raised-hearth fireplace and a beamed ceiling. The kitchen revolves around a center island cooktop and a breakfast nook. The open stairway to the basement is handy and may lead to a future recreation area. In addition to the two full baths, there is an extra wash room. Adjacent is the laundry room and the service entrance from the garage. The blueprints you order for this design will show details for three delightful elevations: a Farmhouse, a Tudor, and a Contemporary.

DESIGN M2565
BEDROOMS 2 or 3 (study)
BATHROOMS 2½
SQUARE FOOTAGE 1,540
PRICE B2

WIDTH 61' 8"
DEPTH 44'

FRONT-PORCH RANCH HOUSE

Whether it's a starter house you are after, or one in which to spend your retirement years, this pleasing Ranch House will provide a full measure of pride in ownership. The contrast of vertical and horizontal lines, the double front doors and the coach lamp post at the garage create an inviting exterior. The floor plan functions in an orderly and efficient manner. The 26-foot gathering room has a delightful view of the rear yard and will take care of those formal dining occasions. There are two full baths serving the three bedrooms. There are plenty of storage facilities, two sets of glass doors to the terraces, a fireplace in the gathering room, a basement and an attached two-car garage to act as a buffer against the wind. In all, a very delightful home.

WIDTH 71' 8"
DEPTH 36'

DESIGN M2597
BEDROOMS 3
BATHROOMS 2
SQUARE FOOTAGE 1,515
PRICE B2

Rustic charm abounds in this delightful 1½-story Ranch House. Vertical wood siding, warm brick, double entry doors and country-style shutters work in concert for a beautiful outside. On the inside is a wonderful floor plan. A large foyer greets family and guests alike and is complemented by a hall bathroom that also serves the master bedroom. The living room and sunken family room are thoughtfully separated, though each has easy access to the kitchen and eating areas. Notice the cozy fireplaces in both gathering areas. The service entrance has a washroom for easy cleanups. Upstairs are three bedrooms and a full bath. Don't miss the walk-in linen closet and storage area on this floor as well.

WIDTH 71' 4"
DEPTH 47' 10"

SECOND FLOOR

FIRST FLOOR

DESIGN	M2500
BEDROOMS	4
BATHROOMS	2½
FIRST FLOOR	1,851 Sq. Ft.
SECOND FLOOR	762 Sq. Ft.
TOTAL	2,613 Sq. Ft.
PRICE	B2

WIDTH 67' 4"
DEPTH 61' 4"

Vertical boards and battens, field-stone, a bay window, a dovecote, a gas lamp, and a recessed front entrance are among the appealing exterior features of this U-shaped Ranch House. Through the double front doors, flanked by glass side lights, is the spacious foyer. Straight ahead is the cozy sunken gathering room with its sloping, beamed ceiling, raised-hearth fireplace and two sets of sliding glass doors to the rear entrance. To the right of the foyer is the sleeping wing with three bedrooms, a study (or fourth bed-room) and two baths. Note that the master bedroom has two vanities, a large dressing area, and bay window. To the left is the strategically located powder room and large kitchen with nook and bay window.

DESIGN	M2527
BEDROOMS	3 or 4
	(study)
BATHROOMS	2½
SQUARE FOOTAGE	2,392
PRICE	B3

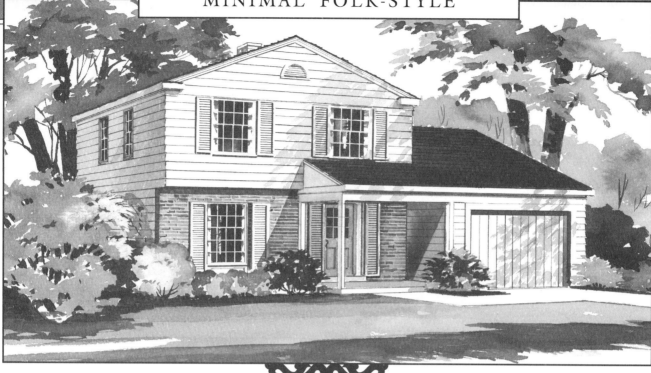

Traditional style is still the favorite of many, as evidenced by the popularity of this two-story Folk-Style Farmhouse. This simple, yet appealing design works well even on narrow lots and still delivers all the livability needed by the active family. A large living room is complemented by a formal dining room placed conveniently near the U-shaped kitchen. The family room, tucked away to the rear of the plan, has sliding glass doors to an outdoor terrace. Notice the half bath on this floor for the convenience of guests. Upstairs are three bedrooms and a full bath. An adequate linen closet in the hallway serves bath storage needs. Though designed for slab foundations, the blueprints for this home also offer an optional basement plan.

FIRST FLOOR

WIDTH 34'
DEPTH 30'

SECOND FLOOR

OPTIONAL BASEMENT

DESIGN M1354
BEDROOMS 3
BATHROOMS 1½
FIRST FLOOR 644 Sq. Ft.
SECOND FLOOR 572 Sq. Ft.
TOTAL 1,216 Sq. Ft.
PRICE B1

FIRST FLOOR

SECOND FLOOR
(4-BEDROOM)

OPTIONAL
3-BEDROOM PLAN

WIDTH 48'
DEPTH 34' 10"

This classic Folk-Style Farmhouse design has the double advantage of good looks and a hardworking floor plan. On the outside, a brick first floor is complemented by wood siding on the second floor. Through the double front doors is a long foyer with coat closet and half bath for guests. To the right is the formal living area with dining room to the rear. The grand kitchen has a pass-through counter to the breakfast room. The sunken family room features a beamed ceiling, built-in bookshelves and warm hearth. Sliding glass doors lead to a full-width rear terrace. Upstairs are four bedrooms (or choose the three-bedroom option included in the blueprint package) and two full baths.

DESIGN M1956
BEDROOMS 3 or 4
BATHROOMS 2½
FIRST FLOOR 990 Sq. Ft.
SECOND FLOOR 728 Sq. Ft.
TOTAL 1,718 Sq. Ft.
PRICE B1

This interesting design combines the rustic appeal of Farmhouse styling with the practicality of multi-level floor planning. The covered front porch leads through double doors to the entry foyer with large coat closet. To the left is a living room with bay window. Opening directly off this room is the formal dining room with another bay. The kitchen has an island cooktop, attached breakfast room, pantry and built-in desk. This area overlooks the family room which is on a lower level. A laundry area with washroom completes the lower levels. Upstairs are three bedrooms plus a master suite with dressing room, huge walk-in closet and full bath. This level also features a private balcony overlooking the terraces below.

MAIN AND LOWER LEVELS

UPPER LEVEL

DESIGN	M2786
BEDROOMS	4
BATHROOMS	2½
MAIN LEVEL	871 Sq. Ft.
UPPER LEVEL	1,132 Sq. Ft.
LOWER LEVEL	528 Sq. Ft.
TOTAL	2,531 Sq. Ft.
PRICE	B2

WIDTH 54'
DEPTH 44' 4"

SECOND FLOOR

WIDTH 70'
DEPTH 34'

This Folk-Style Farmhouse offers plenty of modern comfort with its covered front porch sporting pillars and rails, double chimneys, and four upstairs bedrooms. The first-floor attachment includes a family room with bay window and fireplace. It leads from the main house to a two-car garage through a rear entrance with laundry and sewing room. Formal occasions take place in the living and dining rooms. A U-shaped kitchen with attached breakfast room is fully equipped. The upstairs is accessible from stairs just off the front foyer. Included is a master bedroom suite with dressing room, double vanity and walk-in closet. Three family bedrooms share a full bath.

FIRST FLOOR

DESIGN	M2908
BEDROOMS	4
BATHROOMS	2½
FIRST FLOOR	1,229 Sq. Ft.
SECOND FLOOR	1,153 Sq. Ft.
TOTAL	2,382 Sq. Ft.
PRICE	B2

CLASSIC FARMHOUSE

This masterfully affordable Farm-house manages to include all the basics—then adds a little more. Note the wraparound covered porch, large family room with raised-hearth fireplace and wet bar, spacious kitchen with island cooktop, formal dining room, and rear terrace. Upstairs, the plan is as flexible as they come: three or four bedrooms (the fourth could easily be a study or playroom) and plenty of unfinished attic just waiting to be transformed into living space. This area would make a fine sewing room, home office or children's playroom. Special amenities make this home a stand-out from others in its class. Note the many built-ins, the sliding glass doors to the terrace, and the wealth of closets and storage space.

FIRST FLOOR

SECOND FLOOR

ATTIC

WIDTH 59' 8"
DEPTH 54'

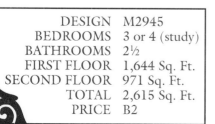

DESIGN	M2945
BEDROOMS	3 or 4 (study)
BATHROOMS	2½
FIRST FLOOR	1,644 Sq. Ft.
SECOND FLOOR	971 Sq. Ft.
TOTAL	2,615 Sq. Ft.
PRICE	B2

TERRACE

GARAGE
11⁴x22⁴

PORCH

DINING RM.
12⁴x11⁰⁺BAY

KITCHEN
12⁰x11⁴

FAMILY DINING
16⁴x11⁴

BRM
CL

MUD ROOM

WASH
RM.

CURB

RAISED HEARTH

THRU-FIREPLACE

RAISED HEARTH

FAMILY LIVING
19⁸x13⁴

PARLOR
14⁴x17⁰

FOYER

COVERED PORCH

FIRST FLOOR

PORCH

The charm of early America is exemplified in this delightful Farmhouse design. Beyond its country-style facade lies a modern vital floor plan. The entry foyer opens the way to formal gatherings. To the left is the parlor with fireplace and formal dining room with bay window. To the right is the comfortable family room with raised-hearth through-fireplace to the casual dining area. A U-shaped kitchen is handy for both living areas. Upstairs are three bedrooms; the master is lavishly appointed with three closets, a dressing room and double vanities. Note the large storage area accessed through the closet. Two family bedrooms share a full bath.

SECOND FLOOR

BATH

STOR

BATH

CEILING CLIP

BEDROOM
18²x8⁰-11⁴

DRESSING RM.

CL

STOR

TOWELS

CL

DN

LIN.

CEILING CLIP

CL

CL

CEILING CLIP

CEILING CLIP

BEDROOM
17⁴x10⁸-13⁴

MASTER BEDROOM
21⁰x9⁴-14⁸

WIDTH 62'
DEPTH 42'

DESIGN	M2681
BEDROOMS	3
BATHROOMS	2½
FIRST FLOOR	1,350 Sq. Ft.
SECOND FLOOR	1,224 Sq. Ft.
TOTAL	2,574 Sq. Ft.
PRICE	B2

Here's a traditional Farmhouse design that's made for down-home hospitality. The star attractions are the large covered porch and terrace. Inside, though, the design is truly a hard worker: separate living and family rooms, each with its own fireplace; formal dining room; large kitchen and breakfast area with bay window; separate study; workshop with plenty of room to maneuver; mud room; and four bedrooms upstairs. The master suite has an amenity-laden bath with window seat, vanity area and His and Hers walk-in closets. Don't miss the other extras throughout the home: curio niches, built-in bookshelves, entry powder room, kitchen pass-through, pantry, planning desk and workbench.

SECOND FLOOR

FIRST FLOOR

DESIGN	M2946
BEDROOMS	4
BATHROOMS	2½+powder rm
FIRST FLOOR	1,590 Sq. Ft.
SECOND FLOOR	1,344 Sq. Ft.
TOTAL	2,934 Sq. Ft.
PRICE	B3

WIDTH 74'
DEPTH 46'

CLASSIC FARMHOUSE

FIRST FLOOR

TERRACE

RAISED HEARTH

FAMILY RM. 21⁴ x 13⁶

BREAKFAST RM. 14⁰ x 11⁶

KITCHEN 10⁰ x 11⁸

DINING RM. 13⁰ x 11⁶ + BAY

LAUNDRY RM. 10⁰ x 7⁶

DRY. WASH. CL. PANTRY

PDR. RM.

CL.

DESK BRM. CL. REF'G OVEN

DN.

CURB

FOYER

LIVING RM. 17⁰ x 13⁶

COVERED PORCH

GARAGE 21⁴ x 21⁸

WIDTH   59' 8"
DEPTH   44'

SECOND FLOOR

BEDROOM / STUDY 11⁰ x 13²

BATH DRESS. RM.

VANITY

MASTER BEDROOM 13⁰ x 13²

CL.

CL.

BATH

DN.

UP TO ATTIC

BATH

CL.

LIN.

BEDROOM 10⁰ x 10⁶

BEDROOM 13⁰ x 10⁶

CL.

ATTIC

ROOF

DN.

ROOF

ATTIC 29⁴ x 26⁴
(HEADROOM 29⁴ x 10⁴)

ROOF

This Classic Farmhouse has all the most up-to-date features expected in a new home. Beginning with the formal areas, this design offers something for the whole family. There is the quiet corner living room which has an opening to the sizable dining room, conveniently located, with the efficient U-shaped kitchen just a step away. The kitchen features many built-ins and a pass-through to the beamed-ceiling breakfast room. Sliding glass doors to the terrace are fine attractions in both the sunken family room and breakfast room. Upstairs are four bedrooms (or make one a study) and two baths, including the master suite with dressing area and double vanity.

DESIGN	M2774
BEDROOMS	3 or 4 (study)
BATHROOMS	2½
FIRST FLOOR	1,370 Sq. Ft.
SECOND FLOOR	969 Sq. Ft.
TOTAL	2,339 Sq. Ft.
PRICE	B2

This two-story Farmhouse faithfully recalls the 18th-Century homestead of Secretary of Foreign Affairs John Jay. However, its floor plan can easily keep pace with the most modern of residences. The large entry foyer features a grand double staircase to the second floor. To the left is an extravagant country kitchen with fireplace and clutter room beyond. The living room with music alcove and fireplace are to the right; the formal dining room connects this room with the kitchen. A quiet library is tucked away in a far wing of the house; it enjoys a third fireplace. Upstairs, there are three comfortable bedrooms. Notice that covered porches grace both the front and rear of this grand home.

FIRST FLOOR

SECOND FLOOR

DESIGN M2694
BEDROOMS 3
BATHROOMS 2½+powder rm
FIRST FLOOR 2,026 Sq. Ft.
SECOND FLOOR 1,386 Sq. Ft.
TOTAL 3,412 Sq. Ft.
PRICE B3

WIDTH 84'
DEPTH 65' 8"

FIRST FLOOR

WIDTH 44' 8"
DEPTH 36'

A covered porch and balcony high-light the facade of this family-oriented Farmhouse design. Inside, a symmetrical floor plan offers the best in family living. Gathering areas dominate the front of the first floor: living room with fireplace to the left and family room with beamed ceiling and wet bar to the right. Directly to the back is the country kitchen with another fireplace and island cooktop. The dining room flanks the kitchen on one side; a convenient laundry room is on the other. Four bedrooms are found on the second floor. The master suite has a curved counter and large walk-in closet in its private bath. Three other bedrooms share a full bath with double vanities.

SECOND FLOOR

DESIGN	M2664
BEDROOMS	4
BATHROOMS	2½
FIRST FLOOR	1,308 Sq. Ft.
SECOND FLOOR	1,262 Sq. Ft.
TOTAL	2,570 Sq. Ft.
PRICE	B2

This appealing Farmhouse is complemented by an inviting front porch. Upon entry, notice the nice-sized study to the right and spacious living room to the left. The adjacent dining room is enriched by an attractive bay window. Just a step away, an efficient kitchen will satisfy the fussiest of cooks. Casual gatherings can be enjoyed in the large family room. The tavern/snack bar makes entertaining a breeze. Upstairs is a master bedroom suite featuring an oversized tub and shower and a dressing room with two closets and a window seat. Each of the other two bedrooms has two dormer windows; the shared bath has one also. Look for abundant storage space in the area over the attic.

FIRST FLOOR

SECOND FLOOR

DESIGN	M2890
BEDROOMS	3
BATHROOMS	2½
FIRST FLOOR	1,612 Sq. Ft.
SECOND FLOOR	1,356 Sq. Ft.
TOTAL	2,968 Sq. Ft.
PRICE	B3

WIDTH 68'
DEPTH 50' 4"

FIRST FLOOR

Dormers and a covered porch are a fine introduction to this two-story Farmhouse. Inside, the appeal is also outstanding. Note the size of the gathering room which is open to the dining room. The cozy fireplace and sliding glass doors to the rear terrace are nice touches. The kitchen/nook area is spacious and features an island cooktop, built-in desk and more. The laundry and service areas are close by for convenience. The master bedroom upstairs has its own cozy fireplace and a bath that pampers. Two family bedrooms share private access to a second full bath. Notice the huge linen closet in the hall.

SECOND FLOOR

WIDTH 82' 8"
DEPTH 34'

DESIGN	M2650
BEDROOMS	3
BATHROOMS	2½
FIRST FLOOR	1,451 Sq. Ft.
SECOND FLOOR	1,091 Sq. Ft.
TOTAL	2,542 Sq. Ft.
PRICE	B2

This board-and-batten Farmhouse has all of the country charm you're looking for. The large front covered porch will be appreciated during warm-weather months. Immediately off the front entrance is the delightful corner living room. The dining room with bay window will be easily served by the U-shaped kitchen. Informal family living takes place in the family room with raised-hearth fireplace, sliding glass doors to the rear terrace, and easy access to the powder room, laundry room and service entrance. The second floor has three bedrooms and two full baths. The master has a dormer and walk-in closet. Two other bedrooms share the second bath.

FIRST FLOOR

WIDTH 61' 4"
DEPTH 38'

SECOND FLOOR

DESIGN   M2776
BEDROOMS   3
BATHROOMS   2½
FIRST FLOOR   1,134 Sq. Ft.
SECOND FLOOR   874 Sq. Ft.
TOTAL   2,008 Sq. Ft.
PRICE   B2

FIRST FLOOR

SECOND FLOOR

WIDTH 90'
DEPTH 42'

A big wraparound covered porch makes the most of this Farmhouse's exterior. On the inside, a well-designed floor plan enhances livability. Up front, flanking the entry foyer, are a living room with fireplace, and a formal dining room. To the rear are a study that could be used as a guest room, and a family room with another fireplace. The kitchen/breakfast room combination is conveniently located near the service entrance of the garage. Three bedrooms are located upstairs. Besides the master with window seat and dressing area, there are two family bedrooms—one with a large walk-in closet. Don't miss the large rear terrace which can be accessed from sliding glass doors in the family room and the study.

DESIGN	M2865
BEDROOMS	3 or 4 (study)
BATHROOMS	3½
FIRST FLOOR	1,703 Sq. Ft.
SECOND FLOOR	1,044 Sq. Ft.
TOTAL	2,747 Sq. Ft.
PRICE	B3

Rustic charm abounds in this pleasant Farmhouse rendition. Covered porches to the front and rear enclose living potential for the whole family. Flanking the entrance foyer are the living and dining rooms. Each is large enough to handle both casual and formal entertaining. To the rear is the L-shaped kitchen with island cook top and snack bar. A small family room/breakfast nook is attached for very informal activities. A private study is tucked away on this floor next to the master suite. On the second floor are three bedrooms and a full bath. Two of the bedrooms have charming dormer windows.

FIRST FLOOR

SECOND FLOOR

DESIGN	M3396
BEDROOMS	4
BATHROOMS	2½
FIRST FLOOR	1,830 Sq. Ft.
SECOND FLOOR	1,012 Sq. Ft.
TOTAL	2,842 Sq. Ft.
PRICE	B3

WIDTH 62'
DEPTH 48'8"

PRAIRIE-STYLE FARMHOUSE

FIRST FLOOR

This is the ultimate in farmhouse living—six dormer windows and a porch that stretches essentially around the entire house. Inside the plan is open and inviting. Besides the large country kitchen with fireplace, there is a small game room with attached tavern, a library with built-in bookshelves and a fireplace, and a formal living room. The second floor has four bedrooms and three full baths. Note the separate His and Hers walk-in closets and the whirlpool spa in the master suite bath. The service entrance features a mud room and laundry area conveniently just off the garage.

SECOND FLOOR

WIDTH 82'
DEPTH 49' 8"

DESIGN	M3399
BEDROOMS	4
BATHROOMS	3½
FIRST FLOOR	1,716 Sq. Ft.
SECOND FLOOR	2,102 Sq. Ft.
TOTAL	3,818 Sq. Ft.
PRICE	B4

Five second-story dormers and a wide covered front porch add to the country charm of this Farmhouse design. Inside, an open floor plan offers great livability. The entry foyer opens to the left to a formal living room with fireplace and attached dining room. To the right is a private study. The back of the plan is dominated by a huge country kitchen featuring an island cook top and access to the rear covered porch. On this floor is the master suite with dual lavatories and a large walk-in closet. The second floor holds three bedrooms (or two and a sitting room) with two full baths. The dormers add interest to rooms on this floor.

FIRST FLOOR

SECOND FLOOR

DESIGN	M3397
BEDROOMS	3 or 4 (sitting room)
BATHS	3½
FIRST FLOOR	1,855 Sq. Ft.
SECOND FLOOR	1,241 Sq. Ft.
TOTAL	3,096 Sq. Ft.
PRICE	B4

WIDTH 82'
DEPTH 50'

FIRST FLOOR

With its classic Farmhouse good-looks and just-right floor plan, this country residence has it all. The wraparound covered porch at the entry gives way to a long foyer with open staircase. To the right and left are the formal dining room and the living room. More casual living areas are to the rear: a family room, and U-shaped kitchen with attached breakfast room. A covered porch at the back is reached by two sets of sliding glass doors. The second floor holds sleeping areas—two family bedrooms and a huge master suite with walk-in closet and pampering master bath. Special amenities include an ample laundry area, large walk-in pantry and corner fireplaces in both living areas.

SECOND FLOOR

WIDTH 92'
DEPTH 44'

DESIGN	M3398
BEDROOMS	3
BATHROOMS	2½
FIRST FLOOR	1,533 Sq. Ft.
SECOND FLOOR	1,288 Sq. Ft.
TOTAL	2,821 Sq. Ft.
PRICE	B3

THE BLUEPRINT PACKAGE

HOME PLANNERS, INC.

Each set of blueprints is an interrelated collection of plans, measurements, drawings and diagrams showing precisely how your house comes together. Here's what the package includes:

- **FRONTAL SHEET.** An artist's landscaped sketch of the exterior along with inkline floor plans.
- **FOUNDATION PLAN.** A complete basement and foundation plan drawn to ¼-inch scale, plus a sample plot plan for locating your house on a building site.
- **DETAILED FLOOR PLANS.** Drawn to ¼-inch scale, each floor plan includes cross-section detail keys and layouts of electrical outlets and switches.
- **HOUSE CROSS-SECTIONS.** Large-scale interior details show key sections of the foundation, interior and exterior walls, floors and roof details.

- **INTERIOR ELEVATIONS.** Large-scale interior details show the design of kitchen cabinets, bathrooms, laundry areas, fireplaces and built-ins.
- **EXTERIOR ELEVATIONS.** Drawings in ¼-inch scale show the front, rear and sides of your house.

SPECIFICATION OUTLINE. Available separately from the blueprint package, this handy 16-page, fill-in-the-blanks document contains more than 150 stages crucial to the construction of your home. A handy guide and record, it allows you to pinpoint building materials, equipment and methods of construction.

MATERIALS LIST. Also available separately, this customized materials list specifies the quantity, type and size of material needed to build your house (with the exception of mechanical-system items).

PRICES

The blueprints you order are a master plan for building your new home. Even the smallest house in the Home Planners' portfolio is a complicated combination of construction and architectural data. Bigger houses, irregularly shaped houses and houses with an abundance of design features are even more complex and require proportionately greater resources to design and develop. The price schedule below takes these factors into account.

	B1	B2	B3	B4	B5
One-set Study Package	$150	$180	$210	$240	$360
Four-set Building Package	$210	$240	$270	$300	$420
Eight-set Building Package	$270	$300	$330	$360	$480
One-set Reproducible Sepias	$300	$360	$420	$480	$600

Additional Identical Blueprints in same order $40 per set
Reverse Blueprints (Mirror-Image) $40 per set
Specification Outlines $5 each

MATERIALS LISTS
Schedule B1-B4 $35 each
Schedule B5 $40 each
Additional Materials Lists in same order $10 each

TO ORDER BLUEPRINTS, TURN TO PAGE 187.

For more information on these plans, write:
Home Planners, Inc., 3275 West Ina Road, Suite 110, Tucson, Arizona 85741

HISTORICAL REPLICATIONS, INC.

In 1977, while living in Atlanta, Cecilia Reese Bullock began a construction company that specialized in building traditional houses. One day a visitor to her job site complimented Bullock on her imaginative incorporation of architectural antiques in the new homes she was building—but lamented the shortage of actual old houses available for purchase and renovation.

"Suddenly I had an idea," Bullock recalls. "If there were not enough old houses for old-house lovers—why not meet the needs of this market by building new houses that retained the exact proportions and details of historic homes—yet incorporated all the latest technological advances in a floor plan updated for modern lifestyles?"

Bullock began planning her next construction project: an exact copy of an 1855 antebellum Farmhouse that she had long admired. She decided to build a replica of this historic home and test her design concept in the heavily attended Home Expo (The Atlanta Homebuilders' Association Parade of Homes).

Bullock remembers that the response to the home was overwhelming. Throughout the entire Expo, long lines remained constant in front of the house. "My doubts were resolved: there was a very receptive and very appreciative market for new houses that were identical to old houses."

Shortly after the Home Expo, Bullock's husband was unexpectedly transferred to Jackson, Mississippi. "As soon as I completed my building projects in Atlanta, I joined my husband in Jackson. I had decided to pursue the historical house-plan concept in earnest. With the assistance of artists, draftsmen and designers both in Jackson and Atlanta, I developed twenty-four Victorian and Farmhouse designs. This first portfolio was so well received that I soon enlarged it to include forty-four designs. And, even though we are known nationally as specialists in Victorian architecture, over the past decade we have developed three other portfolios in Acadian, Greek Revival, Georgian and Federal styles."

Bullock increasingly had to expand her staff to accommodate the demand for alterations and custom designs. "Even though I had originally planned to offer only stock plans, I had so many requests for custom designs that I could not ignore the fact that there was a need for specialized plans to meet individualized needs."

Brian Norris, Executive Vice President of Historical Replications, has been with the firm since its move to Jackson. "I have always enjoyed traditional residential design," says Norris. "I had heard of Historical Replications when I was in architecture school. I thought that the idea of replicating existing exteriors and designing new floor plans was very unique. Immediately upon graduation, I went to work for the firm.

"I have studied Victorians from San Francisco to Savannah," he notes, "and taken countless photographs to insure that our design and drafting staff use only authentic details. Our owners have reported that visitors—and on occasion, subcontractors—have mistaken their new house for a skillful renovation of an old one; we consider that the utmost compliment."

Over the past ten years, Historical Replications has seen its designs featured in most major building magazines. *Traditional Building* magazine described Cecilia Reese Bullock as the person "who has had more influence than any other single individual in making historical American architecture popular in the new housing market." In 1990, Bullock was recognized for her contributions to American residential architecture in the prestigious British documentary series "Hooray for Today, USA."

Comments Bullock: "Brian and I are dedicated to developing designs that preserve not only the ambience but the *quality* of the past era. And though our floor plans incorporate the latest amenities, our houses convey the feeling of a beloved old home. They create an emotional, nostalgic response."

QUEEN ANNE COTTAGE

With a facade and floor plan reminiscent of an earlier era, this charming Victorian house unobtrusively incorporates such modern amenities as a powder room, a separate breakfast bay and a walk-through laundry room. The foyer opens onto a well-proportioned great room with a wood-burning fireplace. A large cased opening leads to the adjacent dining room. A double tier of windows illuminates the dramatic stairwell, which leads up to three bedrooms. The master suite is carefully zoned away from the other two bedrooms; it contains a compartmentalized dressing area and an oversized closet. The luxurious master bath features His and Hers vanities. Plans for the detached garages for this home can be seen on pages 176 and 177.

FIRST FLOOR

SECOND FLOOR

WIDTH 27'
DEPTH 47'

DESIGN	M8800
BEDROOMS	3
BATHROOMS	2½
FIRST FLOOR	846 Sq. Ft.
SECOND FLOOR	784 Sq. Ft.
TOTAL	1,630 Sq. Ft.
PRICE	C1

FOLK VICTORIAN COTTAGE

BREAKFAST

GREAT ROOM
13-6 x 19-0

KITCHEN

DINING ROOM
10-0 12-0

LIVING ROOM
13-0 15-6

UP

FIRST FLOOR

BEDROOM
10-0 x 11-6

BEDROOM
11-0 11-6

DOWN

MASTER BEDROOM
13-0 15-6

SECOND FLOOR

The inviting porch of this charming turn-of-the-century house extends a gracious welcome. The expansive foyer opens onto both the living room and great room, which contain fireplaces. A formal dining room is conveniently situated between the living room and the kitchen, and is well located for entertaining. The master bedroom has a bath with a double vanity and a separate shower stall, as well as an oversized whirlpool tub. A large walk-in closet completes the amenities of this spacious room. The other bedrooms open directly into a compartmentalized bath with another double vanity. This house is especially suitable for a narrow lot and is compatible with a detached garage, plans for which can be seen on pages 176 and 177.

DESIGN	M8801
BEDROOMS	3
BATHROOMS	2½
FIRST FLOOR	1,066 Sq. Ft.
SECOND FLOOR	913 Sq. Ft.
TOTAL	1,979 Sq. Ft.
PRICE	C1

WIDTH 31'
DEPTH 50'

This delightful Victorian design is an updated version of an authentic turn-of-the-century design. Originally offered in George Barber's 1890 plan book, *The Cottage Souvenir #3,* this appealing house readily adapts itself to a more modern floor plan. The expansive kitchen, with an attached island and breakfast bar, is a welcome addition to the original plan. A walk-in utility room, located conveniently near the kitchen, facilitates laundry chores. A cozy fireplace warms the great room. The second-floor master suite features a walk-in closet, a separate sitting area and a large master bath with individual vanities. Both bedrooms contain generous walk-in closets. Plans for detached garages for this home can be seen on pages 176 and 177.

DINING ROOM
11-6 x 13-0

LAUNDRY

KITCHEN

GREAT ROOM
13-0 x 19-0

UP

FIRST FLOOR

BEDROOM
12-6 x 13-6

MASTER
BEDROOM
13-0 x 13-6

DOWN

SITTING
ROOM
7-6 x 9-0

SECOND FLOOR

DESIGN	M8802
BEDROOMS	2
BATHROOMS	2½
FIRST FLOOR	828 Sq. Ft.
SECOND FLOOR	700 Sq. Ft.
TOTAL	1,528 Sq. Ft.
PRICE	C1

WIDTH   30'
DEPTH   34'

FIRST FLOOR

WIDTH 38'
DEPTH 42'

SECOND FLOOR

Undeniably appealing, the wraparound porch of this engaging dwelling lends additional warmth to a very special house plan. Within, a graceful stairway rises from a spacious foyer and is brightened through thoughtful window placement. The great room features a fireplace and plenty of space for entertaining. The adjoining formal dining room opens onto a sheltered porch. Additional seating space for less formal dining is offered in the large breakfast bay. Nearby, a built-in cabinet provides shelves for cookbooks and cherished serving pieces. Upstairs floorspace is especially well-utilized. A minimum amount of hallway is used to provide access to the three bedrooms. The master suite has a partitioned bath and a separate tub and shower. Plans for detached garages for this home can be seen on pages 176 and 177.

DESIGN	M8806
BEDROOMS	3
BATHROOMS	2½
FIRST FLOOR	1,005 Sq. Ft.
SECOND FLOOR	846 Sq. Ft.
TOTAL	1,851 Sq. Ft.
PRICE	C1

FOLK VICTORIAN COTTAGE

This nostalgic house is an adaptation of the common T-shaped Farmhouses that ornament the nation's countryside. The front door is encircled by glass sidelights and a transom that contribute light to the sparkling entryway. An especially spacious great room is well-lit from long windows that, when opened, will provide ample air circulation on moderate days. A step-in pantry allows plenty of storage space for the cook who likes to shop ahead. On the second floor, an open railing overlooks the stairs below. The master bath includes a whirlpool tub and a separate shower. Plans for detached garages for this home can be seen on pages 176 and 177.

FIRST FLOOR

SECOND FLOOR

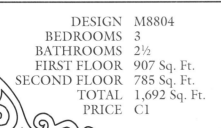

DESIGN	M8804
BEDROOMS	3
BATHROOMS	2½
FIRST FLOOR	907 Sq. Ft.
SECOND FLOOR	785 Sq. Ft.
TOTAL	1,692 Sq. Ft.
PRICE	C1

WIDTH 36'
DEPTH 31'

QUEEN ANNE

BREAKFAST

GREAT ROOM
16-0 x 17-0

UP   **KITCHEN**

MASTER BEDROOM
14-0 x 16-0

FIRST FLOOR

BEDROOM
10-6 x 11-6

BEDROOM
10-6 x 11-6

LAUNDRY

BEDROOM
9-6 x 12-6   **DOWN**

BEDROOM
12-0 x 14-0

SECOND FLOOR

Well suited for a narrow lot, this splendid home contains authentic Queen Anne detailing with an asymmetrical facade and dominant front-facing gable. Within, a very open floor plan furnishes the right setting for today's more informal lifestyles. A first-floor master suite offers plenty of privacy in this five-bedroom home. On the second floor, the bedroom at the top of the stairs could easily be adapted to serve as a playroom or study. The front bedroom on the second floor has a balcony that could easily be enclosed if a more spacious bedroom is desired. This versatile plan is perfect for the larger family desiring an affordably priced house. Plans for detached garages for this home can be seen on pages 176 and 177.

WIDTH 29'
DEPTH 46'

DESIGN	M8811
BEDROOMS	5
BATHROOMS	3½
FIRST FLOOR	1,026 Sq. Ft.
SECOND FLOOR	937 Sq. Ft.
TOTAL	1,963 Sq. Ft.
PRICE	C1

FOLK VICTORIAN COTTAGE

The lacy and decorative ornamentation of this romantic cottage is a commonly observed feature of homes of the Victorian era. The bayed dining room on the front of the house echoes the original floor plan; but the up-to-date kitchen with its convenient breakfast bar introduces the latest technologic advances. A long, narrow pantry provides ample storage for food and for odd-size serving pieces. The first-floor master suite is a most welcome feature. The master bath features His and Hers vanities, as well as both a tub and separate shower. Upstairs, three spacious bedrooms house large closets. Additional storage space is provided in the walk-out attic. Plans for detached garages for this home can be seen on pages 176 and 177.

FIRST FLOOR

SECOND FLOOR

DESIGN	M8803
BEDROOMS	4
BATHROOMS	2
FIRST FLOOR	1,192 Sq. Ft.
SECOND FLOOR	728 Sq. Ft.
TOTAL	1,920 Sq. Ft.
PRICE	C1

WIDTH 35'
DEPTH 46'

FIRST FLOOR

BREAKFAST

GREAT ROOM
14-6 x 18-6

UP

KITCHEN

DINING ROOM
11-0 x 12-0

MASTER
BEDROOM
12-6 x 14-6

Some houses possess more than their fair share of warmth and charm, and this captivating design belongs in that category. The wraparound porch is a design element that is irresistibly inviting. A front-facing gable with fishscale shingles and gingerbread ornament imparts additional excitement. The master bedroom, located on the first floor, features a supersized closet. A pass-through from the kitchen to the great room includes the cook in the midst of family life. Ascending conveniently from the great room, the stairs lead up to three bedrooms. A spacious dressing area with two separate vanities and multiple linen closets makes sharing a bath easy. Plans for detached garages for this home can be seen on pages 176 and 177.

BEDROOM
11-0 x 11-0

BEDROOM
11-0 x 12-6

DOWN

BEDROOM
11-0 x 12-6

SECOND FLOOR

WIDTH 44'
DEPTH 51'

DESIGN	M8810
BEDROOMS	4
BATHROOMS	2½
FIRST FLOOR	1,240 Sq. Ft.
SECOND FLOOR	718 Sq. Ft.
TOTAL	1,958 Sq. Ft.
PRICE	C1

With its bedazzling windows and intricate exterior details, this spirited Queen Anne residence proclaims its San Francisco heritage. The foyer is open to the second-floor ceiling, creating additional pizazz. Niches are built into the cased opening that leads into the dining room, providing an opportunity to display beloved collections. Openness is achieved with an oversized kitchen, bayed breakfast nook and commodious great room with fireplace. On the second floor, both family bedrooms have walk-in closets and individual vanities; one also features a bay window. The master bedroom suite provides the utmost privacy with its compartmentalized bath. Plans for detached garages for this home can be seen on pages 176 and 177.

FIRST FLOOR

LNDRY

GREAT ROOM
16-6 x 16-6

BREAKFAST

KITCHEN

DINING ROOM
10-6 x 12-0

UP

SECOND FLOOR

BEDROOM
10-6 x 12-0

BEDROOM
10-6 x 14-6

DOWN

MASTER BEDROOM
10-6 x 16-0

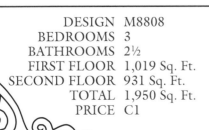

DESIGN	M8808
BEDROOMS	3
BATHROOMS	2½
FIRST FLOOR	1,019 Sq. Ft.
SECOND FLOOR	931 Sq. Ft.
TOTAL	1,950 Sq. Ft.
PRICE	C1

WIDTH 30'
DEPTH 42'

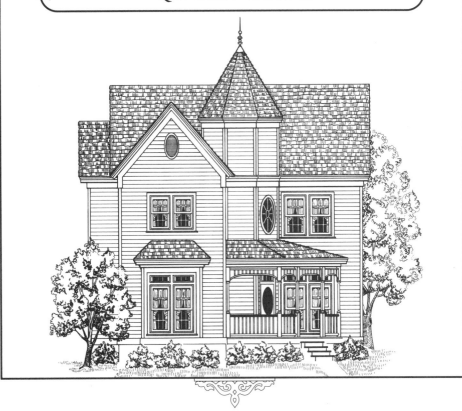

The octagonal foyer of this Queen Anne Style house sets the pace for this enticing Victorian design. This spacious foyer leads to a formal dining room of expansive proportions, and also opens into a great room warmed by a wood-burning fireplace. The stairway arises conveniently near family living areas and ends on a second-floor landing that echoes the octagonal foyer below. Upstairs, a sumptuous master suite features a dazzling bath with a step-up whirlpool tub and separate shower. The oversized master closet contributes ample storage for clothes and accessories. Plans for detached garages for this home can be seen on pages 176 and 177.

BREAKFAST

UP

GREAT ROOM
14-6 X 20-0

LAUN

KITCHEN

DINING ROOM
13-0 X 13-6

FIRST FLOOR

BEDROOM
9-6 X 11-0

MASTER
BEDROOM
14-6 X 15-0

DOWN

BEDROOM
11-6 X 12-6

WIDTH 38'
DEPTH 40'

SECOND FLOOR

DESIGN	M8809
BEDROOMS	3
BATHROOMS	2½
FIRST FLOOR	999 Sq. Ft.
SECOND FLOOR	948 Sq. Ft.
TOTAL	1,947 Sq. Ft.
PRICE	C1

The homes of the Victorian era contain indisputably the most interesting foyers of any architectural period. Frequently, these entry rooms were large enough to serve as auxiliary living spaces for the large families that occupied them. The bayed foyer of this authentic Queen Anne design is ample enough for a cozy sitting area, or, furnished with a desk, a spot for a convenient study. Directly over the foyer, the master bath repeats the bay windows below. This sumptuous bath features an enormous amount of counter space, as well as a whirlpool tub and separate shower. A laundry chute in the master closet places clothes in the huge laundry room directly below. Plans for detached garages for this home can be seen on pages 176 and 177.

FIRST FLOOR

SECOND FLOOR

WIDTH 37'
DEPTH 44'

DESIGN	M8812
BEDROOMS	3
BATHROOMS	2½
FIRST FLOOR	1,118 Sq. Ft.
SECOND FLOOR	1,040 Sq. Ft.
TOTAL	2,158 Sq. Ft.
PRICE	C2

GREAT ROOM
15-0 x 19-0

KITCHEN

LAUN

UP

FIRST FLOOR

DINING ROOM
11-6 x 14-6

Especially suited for a narrow lot, this winning design proclaims its Victorian heritage with appropriately detailed window trim and gable ornaments. A beveled-glass front door opens into a foyer which is illuminated by the three windows on the stairwell. The generous kitchen offers both a breakfast bar on the island and a breakfast nook with built-in seating, if desired. The spacious master bedroom suite features His and Hers walk-in closets. The large master bath with its garden tub is dazzling. Plans for detached garages for this home can be seen on pages 176 and 177.

SECOND FLOOR

BEDROOM
10-6 x 13-0

BEDROOM
11-0 x 13-6

DOWN

MASTER BEDROOM
14-6 x 15-6

WIDTH 31'
DEPTH 36'

DESIGN	M8813
BEDROOMS	3
BATHROOMS	2½
FIRST FLOOR	991 Sq. Ft.
SECOND FLOOR	895 Sq. Ft.
TOTAL	1,886 Sq. Ft.
PRICE	C1

FOLK VICTORIAN

An immense great room is the focal point of this appealing dwelling. This room leads into a large dining room and adjacent kitchen. The long breakfast bar will appeal to families who must catch a quick meal on the run. Nearby, a back entry opens onto a powder room and a walk-through laundry room, a location important to families who need a mudroom as they enter the house. The expansive great room contains a fireplace. The first-floor master suite is isolated from the three upstairs bedrooms. An over-sized tub is a notable feature of the compartmentalized bathroom, as well as a separate shower and His and Hers vanities. Plans for detached garages for this home can be seen on pages 176 and 177.

FIRST FLOOR

LAUN

STOR

DINING ROOM
11-0 X12-6

KITCHEN

GREAT ROOM
16-0 x 20-0

MASTER
BEDROOM
13-0 X 15-0

UP

SECOND FLOOR

BEDROOM
11-6 X 12-6

DOWN

BEDROOM
11-6 X 13-0

BEDROOM
10-0 X 12-0

DESIGN	M8814
BEDROOMS	4
BATHROOMS	2½
FIRST FLOOR	1,168 Sq. Ft.
SECOND FLOOR	672 Sq. Ft.
TOTAL	1,840 Sq. Ft.
PRICE	C1

WIDTH 38'
DEPTH 40'

HISTORICAL REPLICATIONS, INC.

FOLK VICTORIAN

BREAKFAST

DINING ROOM
12-0 x 13-6

KITCHEN

FIRST FLOOR

GREAT ROOM
14-0 x 19-0

MASTER BEDROOM
12-6 x 18-6

UP

BEDROOM
11-6 x 12-6

SITTING AREA

SECOND FLOOR

DOWN

BEDROOM
12-6 x 15-6

OPEN TO BELOW

WIDTH 44'
DEPTH 40'

The front-facing pediment with authentic Victorian sunburst ornamentation crowns the entryway with its oval beveled-glass door. The vaulted or coved ceiling of the great room and dining room contributes a feeling of spaciousness to rooms already generous in proportion. A kitchen with long counters and tall cabinets is adjacent to a walk-in laundry and a deep pantry. The first-floor master suite is exceptionally roomy and contains a compartmentalized bath and walk-in closet. The second-floor bedrooms feature large closets and share a cozy sitting area at the top of the open stairway. Plans for detached garages for this home can be seen on pages 176 and 177.

DESIGN	M8815
BEDROOMS	3
BATHROOMS	2½
FIRST FLOOR	1,424 Sq. Ft.
SECOND FLOOR	689 Sq. Ft.
TOTAL	2,113 Sq. Ft.
PRICE	C2

The front porch of this charming Victorian design, with its turned columns and graceful fretwork, emanates a warm welcome to all who enter. Within, this unpretentious design offers a very open floor plan for those who enjoy a casual lifestyle. The kitchen, breakfast area, and cozy keeping area with fireplace are all one large room. On the opposite side of the center hall, another lengthy room provides the opportunity for additional living and dining areas. A first-floor master suite with a walk-in closet offers both convenience and quiet seclusion. Two second-floor bedrooms share a spacious bath with a double vanity. Plans for detached garages for this home can be seen on pages 176 and 177.

FIRST FLOOR

MASTER BEDROOM
15-0 x 16-0

DINING ROOM
12-0 x 14-6

KITCHEN

GREAT ROOM
14-0 x 14-6

BREAKFAST

KEEPING ROOM

UP

SECOND FLOOR

DOWN

BEDROOM
12-0 x 14-6

BEDROOM
12-0 x 14-6

DESIGN	M8805
BEDROOMS	3
BATHROOMS	2½
FIRST FLOOR	1,490 Sq. Ft.
SECOND FLOOR	610 Sq. Ft.
TOTAL	2,100 Sq. Ft.
PRICE	C2

WIDTH 42'
DEPTH 62'

SECOND FLOOR

BEDROOM
11-6 x 12-0

DOWN

BEDROOM
12-0 x 13-6

STORAGE

STORAGE

STORAGE

FIRST FLOOR

BREAKFAST

MASTER BEDROOM
14-0 x 17-0

KITCHEN

GREAT ROOM
15-6 x 19-6

UP

DINING ROOM
13-0 x 14-6

WIDTH 48'
DEPTH 40'

Asymmetry of facade is a characteristic Victorian feature. Differing wall textures, such as the change from lap siding to fishscale shingles on the front-facing gable, is another distinguishing architectural trait. This inviting dwelling opens into a foyer sparkling with light from a stained-glass window on the stair landing above. A formal dining room and spacious great room provide ample space for holiday festivities. An isolated first-floor master suite offers a handsome bath with separate vanities and a walk-in closet. Above are the two bedrooms with private baths. A large storage area may be completed and used as a third bedroom or a recreational area. Plans for detached garages for this home can be seen on pages 176 and 177.

DESIGN	M8820
BEDROOMS	3 or 4
BATHROOMS	3½
FIRST FLOOR	1,582 Sq. Ft.
SECOND FLOOR	720 Sq. Ft.
TOTAL	2,302 Sq. Ft.
PRICE	C2

Perfect for a narrow lot, this compact design restates its Victorian heritage with a graceful wraparound veranda. The bracketed fretwork which connects the simple columns and frames the long front windows is authentic turn-of-the-century enhancement. An extra-spacious foyer offers access to the long and wide great room and adjacent dining room, which are separated by a generous cased opening. The interior fretwork used here is typical of the period. The breakfast and dining rooms are each flooded with light from their many windows. A large laundry room has a utility sink and plenty of counter space for folding clothes. Above, the commodious master suite features a whirlpool tub crowned with a Palladian window. Each of the bedrooms has a walk-in closet. Plans for detached garages for this home can be seen on pages 176 and 177.

FIRST FLOOR

SECOND FLOOR

DESIGN	M8816
BEDROOMS	3
BATHROOMS	2½
FIRST FLOOR	1,107 Sq. Ft.
SECOND FLOOR	1,039 Sq. Ft.
TOTAL	2,146 Sq. Ft.
PRICE	C2

WIDTH 31'
DEPTH 50'

FIRST FLOOR

LAUNDRY

BREAKFAST

KITCHEN

GREAT ROOM
14-6 x 15-0

UP

DINING ROOM
11-0 x 13-6

LIVING ROOM
10-0 x 17-0

WIDTH 30'
DEPTH 45'

SECOND FLOOR

BEDROOM
11-6 x 13-6

BEDROOM
11-6 x 13-6

DOWN

MASTER BEDROOM
11-6 x 17-0

Adapted from Bicknell's *Detail Cottage and Construction Architecture,* published in 1873, this delightful Victorian residence readily adapts to an up-to-date floor plan. The chief adornment of the elegant foyer is an open stairway. The lengthy formal living room is connected to a spacious dining room, providing excellent circulation for families who enjoy frequent entertaining. The bayed great room contains plans for a built-in bookcase and media center, as well as a closet for game or hobby storage. The open kitchen features a center island with range and a bayed breakfast area. Upstairs, the master suite features a roomy bath with tub and shower and an oversized closet. Plans for detached garages for this home can be seen on pages 176 and 177.

DESIGN	M8817
BEDROOMS	3
BATHROOMS	2½
FIRST FLOOR	1,105 Sq. Ft.
SECOND FLOOR	979 Sq. Ft.
TOTAL	2,084 Sq. Ft.
PRICE	C2

The exuberant visual display created by this delectable Queen Anne design heralds its Victorian heritage. Transom-topped windows accurately reflect the love of views and veneration of sunlight of this era. Inside, a sizable foyer leads into both formal and informal areas. A spacious great room is amply illuminated by a bay encircled with windows. It opens into a sunlit breakfast area that adjoins a well-appointed kitchen with island cooktop. The walk-through laundry is convenient to the kitchen and the outdoors. Above, a capacious master suite has both a whirlpool tub and an elongated shower. The other two bedrooms each have a bay window. Plans for detached garages for this home can be seen on pages 176 and 177.

FIRST FLOOR

KITCHEN

LAUN

BREAKFAST

DINING ROOM
13-0 X 15-6

GREAT ROOM
15-6 x 21-0

LIVING ROOM
12-0 X 14-0

UP

MASTER BEDROOM
15-6 X 19-0

BEDROOM
12-6 X 15-6

DOWN

SECOND FLOOR

BEDROOM
12-0 X 12-6

DESIGN	M8823
BEDROOMS	3
BATHROOMS	2½
FIRST FLOOR	1,325 Sq. Ft.
SECOND FLOOR	1,052 Sq. Ft.
TOTAL	2,377 Sq. Ft.
PRICE	C2

WIDTH 42'
DEPTH 48'

FIRST FLOOR

GREAT ROOM
11-0 x 15-6

MASTER BEDROOM
11-0 x 15-6

KITCHEN

UP

DINING ROOM
11-0 x 12-0

LIVING ROOM
11-0 x 14-0

SECOND FLOOR

STUDY
9-6 x 12-0

BEDROOM
11-0 x 12-0

BEDROOM
11-0 x 12-0

DOWN

WIDTH 36'
DEPTH 40'

This multi-gabled Victorian achieves a formal interior in a compact amount of space. Its nearly square shape makes it surprisingly economical to construct as well as to heat and cool. Four bay windows impart light and drama to the downstairs rooms. An open foyer with an elegant stairwell opens into spacious rooms. The great room features a fireplace and a door to the outside. Zoned quietly away from the noise of family living, the roomy master suite has a bay-windowed sitting area and a spacious bath. Above, two additional bedrooms share a study or a playroom, which could double as a guest room if additional sleeping space is required. Plans for detached garages for this home can be seen on pages 176 and 177.

DESIGN	M8807
BEDROOMS	3 or 4 (study)
BATHROOMS	2½
FIRST FLOOR	1,217 Sq. Ft.
SECOND FLOOR	620 Sq. Ft.
TOTAL	1,837 Sq. Ft.
PRICE	C1

The popular Victorian architect, Shoppell, was the progenitor of this delightful design; the exterior of this house is faithfully reproduced from his book of house plans, *Turn of the Century Houses, Cottages, and Villas.* The sheltering front porch provides cover for the front door and wraps around to provide access to a handy kitchen door. A wide foyer leads to an expansive great room. Just beyond the great room, the dining room connects to the spacious kitchen and breakfast area. Right above the rear porch, a private terrace opens off the master bedroom. The master bath features a large walk-in closet, a double vanity, and separate tub and shower. Two additional bedrooms share a partitioned bath. Plans for detached garages for this home can be seen on pages 176 and 177.

FIRST FLOOR

LAUN

BREAKFAST

DINING ROOM
13-0 x 14-0

KITCHEN

GREAT ROOM
13-6 x 21-6

UP

DESIGN	M8818
BEDROOMS	3
BATHROOMS	2½
FIRST FLOOR	1,085 Sq. Ft.
SECOND FLOOR	1,090 Sq. Ft.
TOTAL	2,175 Sq. Ft.
PRICE	C2

WIDTH 35'
DEPTH 45'

MASTER
BEDROOM
13-0 x 16-6

BEDROOM
11-0 x 13-0

DOWN

SECOND FLOOR

BEDROOM
13-0 x 13-6

QUEEN ANNE

FIRST FLOOR

DINING ROOM
14-0 x 16-0

KITCHEN

GREAT ROOM
13-0 x 20-0

BREAKFAST

UP

SECOND FLOOR

BEDROOM
12-0 x 14-0

BEDROOM
12-0 x 14-0

DOWN

MASTER
BEDROOM
13-0 x 20-0

WIDTH 42'
DEPTH 42'

Sparkling like a jewel with its many beveled-glass transoms, this enticing Queen Anne Victorian delivers the enchantment of living in an authentic turn-of-the-century home. The octagonal tower is surrounded by a wraparound porch featuring the delicate spindlework common to this era. Within, a wide foyer provides a glimpse of the bayed dining room. A rear porch is located behind the great room. An exceptionally large kitchen with a center island opens into the octagonal breakfast bay. On the second floor, the master bath has a step-up whirlpool tub. A private terrace opening off the master suite provides an opportunity for outdoor living, or, if glassed-in, a secluded study. Plans for detached garages for this home can be seen on pages 176 and 177.

DESIGN	M8819
BEDROOMS	3
BATHROOMS	2½
FIRST FLOOR	1,148 Sq. Ft.
SECOND FLOOR	1,095 Sq. Ft.
TOTAL	2,243 Sq. Ft.
PRICE	C2

The lacy spindlework and corner bracket detailing of the inviting front porch announce the Queen Anne heritage of this enchanting design. From the foyer, a U-shaped stairway with a landing window rises gracefully. The living room provides a secluded spot away from the noise of family living, and could easily serve as a quiet study. The roomy kitchen with its work island is connected to a large dining room by a butler's pantry. If desired, a wet bar could be installed here. Above, a generously sized master bedroom offers such amenities as a whirlpool tub and elongated shower stall. Plans for detached garages for this home can be seen on pages 176 and 177.

BREAKFAST

KITCHEN   **LAUN**

DINING ROOM
13-0 X 15-0

GREAT ROOM
15-0 X 18-0

FIRST FLOOR

UP

**LIVING
ROOM**
11-0 X 13-0

BEDROOM
13-0 X 14-6

MASTER BEDROOM
13-0 x 18-0

SECOND FLOOR

BEDROOM
11-0 X 13-0

DESIGN	M8822
BEDROOMS	3
BATHROOMS	2½
FIRST FLOOR	1,259 Sq. Ft.
SECOND FLOOR	1,025 Sq. Ft.
TOTAL	2,284 Sq. Ft.
PRICE	C2

WIDTH 42'
DEPTH 44'

FOLK VICTORIAN

BREAKFAST

GREAT ROOM
16-0 x 20-6

FIRST FLOOR

KITCHEN

DINING ROOM
12-0 x 14-0

GUEST BEDROOM
12-0 x 13-0

UP

This warm and charming house, with its hipped-roof double dormer, is a nostalgic tribute to a beloved architectural era. An inviting porch leads into a traditional foyer; to the left, a spacious dining room opens onto a well-designed kitchen. The great room is warmed by a fireplace flanked with built-in bookcases. The first-floor guest bedroom could also serve as a quiet study. Above, the master bedroom suite includes separate His and Hers closets. The sumptuous master bath has a step-up tub and an oversized shower stall. The two upstairs bedrooms, each with its own walk-in closet, share a luxurious compartmentalized bath featuring separate dressing areas with vanities. Plans for detached garages for this home can be seen on pages 176 and 177.

MASTER BEDROOM
13-0 x 17-0

LAUNDRY

DOWN

SECOND FLOOR

BEDROOM
12-0 x 13-6

BEDROOM
12-0 x 13-6

WIDTH 34'
DEPTH 54'

DESIGN	M8826
BEDROOMS	4
BATHROOMS	3
FIRST FLOOR	1,224 Sq. Ft.
SECOND FLOOR	1,174 Sq. Ft.
TOTAL	2,398 Sq. Ft.
PRICE	C2

QUEEN ANNE

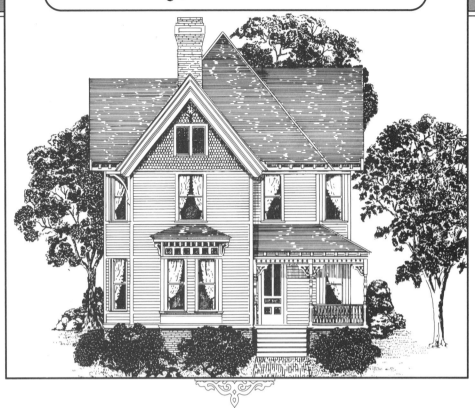

Adapted from the 1890 house plan book *The Cottage Souvenir #2* by the renowned Victorian architect, George Barber, this design graces streets in all parts of the country. Its familiar Queen Anne roof line features a steeply pitched hip roof of irregular shape, with a dominant front-facing gable. Another authentic feature is the wraparound veranda. This updated rendition is perfect for a narrow lot. Formal living and dining areas offer privacy from the family living spaces. The bayed great room features a fireplace with built-in shelves on each side. Above, the master suite contains a bayed sitting area, a walk-in closet and a luxurious bath. The other upstairs bedrooms are exceptionally spacious as well. Plans for detached garages for this home can be seen on pages 176 and 177.

FIRST FLOOR

SECOND FLOOR

WIDTH 34'
DEPTH 49'

DESIGN	M8821
BEDROOMS	3
BATHROOMS	2½
FIRST FLOOR	1,188 Sq. Ft.
SECOND FLOOR	1,133 Sq. Ft.
TOTAL	2,321 Sq. Ft.
PRICE	C2

BREAKFAST

KEEPING ROOM
13-6 X 16-6

KITCHEN

FIRST FLOOR

GREAT ROOM
13-6 X 17-0

UP

DINING ROOM
12-0 X 15-0

The front-facing gables of this hipped-roof Queen Anne, complete with detailed gable ornamentation, proclaim the authenticity of this resplendent design. The pedimented entryway is another architectural characteristic of the Victorian era. Within, a roomy foyer opens into a great room that is flanked by both front and rear porches. The kitchen provides an angled breakfast bar and a cozy keeping room for family members who like to gather during meal preparation. Above, four spacious bedrooms are zoned quietly away from family living. The master suite provides a partitioned bath and walk-in closet. The second-floor laundry saves many a trip up and down the stairs. Plans for detached garages for this home can be seen on pages 176 and 177.

SECOND FLOOR

BEDROOM
11-0 X 13-0

BEDROOM
11-6 X 13-0

DOWN

MASTER
BEDROOM
13-6 X 17-0

LAUN

BEDROOM
12-0 X 15-0

WIDTH 42'
DEPTH 42'

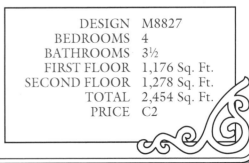

DESIGN	M8827
BEDROOMS	4
BATHROOMS	3½
FIRST FLOOR	1,176 Sq. Ft.
SECOND FLOOR	1,278 Sq. Ft.
TOTAL	2,454 Sq. Ft.
PRICE	C2

Porches that wrap around the outside of a house add special warmth and welcome to the exterior appearance. This appealing dwelling continues its gracious statement with an inviting living room and adjoining dining room. The exceptionally large great room provides a central area for family living, well away from these quieter areas. A country kitchen with a large center work island and breakfast bar allows plenty of company for the family cook. The spacious utility room with a separate laundry sink is convenient to the outdoors and can function as a mudroom. On the second floor, the master suite provides a walk-in closet, separate tub and shower and a double vanity. Plans for detached garages for this home can be seen on pages 176 and 177.

FIRST FLOOR

SECOND FLOOR

DESIGN	M8824
BEDROOMS	3
BATHROOMS	2½
FIRST FLOOR	1,476 Sq. Ft.
SECOND FLOOR	912 Sq. Ft.
TOTAL	2,388 Sq. Ft.
PRICE	C2

WIDTH 58'
DEPTH 51'

KITCHEN   LAUNDRY

BREAKFAST   PANTRY

GREAT ROOM
14-6 x 18-0

FIRST FLOOR

UP

DINING ROOM
12-0 x 12-6

LIVING ROOM
12-0 x 15-0

MASTER
BEDROOM
12-6 x 16-6

Queen Anne houses, with their projecting bays, towers and wrap-around porches, are the apex of the Victorian era. This up-to-date rendition of the beloved style captures a floor plan that is as dramatic within as without. The front-facing pediment ornamented with typical gable detailing highlights the front doorway and provides additional welcome to this enchanting abode. The angles and bays that occur in every first-floor room add visual excitement to formal and informal living and dining areas. A well-lit breakfast bay with its soaring ceiling is a spectacular addition to this classic plan. The first-floor master suite features two walk-in closets. Three upstairs bedrooms also have spacious walk-in closets. Plans for detached garages for this home can be seen on pages 176 and 177.

SECOND FLOOR

BEDROOM
10-0 x 12-6

BEDROOM
12-0 x 15-6

DOWN

BEDROOM
10-0 x 12-6

WIDTH 45'
DEPTH 54'

DESIGN	M8825
BEDROOMS	4
BATHROOMS	3½
FIRST FLOOR	1,600 Sq. Ft.
SECOND FLOOR	790 Sq. Ft.
TOTAL	2,390 Sq. Ft.
PRICE	C2

One of the hallmarks of authentic Victorian architecture is a profusion of windows in a variety of styles. Turn-of-the-century homebuilders repeatedly produced architectural excitement through the creative use of window glass. The transom-topped and side-lighted front door leads into a foyer; a beveled-glass window from the stair landing far above casts jewel-like tones into the area below. An expansive great room has a separate nook that occupies the base of the tower. A covered rear porch provides outdoor living space. Upstairs, the master bedroom also utilizes the tower to provide a separate sitting area. The other two bedrooms are connected via a compartmentalized bath. Plans for detached garages for this home can be seen on pages 176 and 177.

FIRST FLOOR

DESIGN	M8828
BEDROOMS	3
BATHROOMS	2½
FIRST FLOOR	1,349 Sq. Ft.
SECOND FLOOR	1,170 Sq. Ft.
TOTAL	2,519 Sq. Ft.
PRICE	C2

WIDTH 54'
DEPTH 47'

SECOND FLOOR

QUEEN ANNE

FIRST FLOOR

LAUNDRY

BREAKFAST

GREAT ROOM
16-0 x 19-0

PANTRY

KITCHEN

UP

DINING
ROOM
11-0 x 14-0

SITTING
AREA

SECOND FLOOR

MASTER BEDROOM
16-0 x 19-0

BEDROOM
11-0 x 12-0

DOWN

BEDROOM
11-0 x 13-0

WIDTH 44'
DEPTH 46'

The 1878 edition of *Bicknell's Victorian Buildings* inspired the intricate window casings and porch details of this dazzling residence. A tower large enough for a sitting area lends instant impact to the foyer. A charming niche, suitable for either cookbooks or collectibles, is tucked between the great room and breakfast area; a glassed-door hutch built into the breakfast room provides additional space for storage and display. The bayed kitchen with work island and walk-in pantry provides all the latest amenities. Above, the guest bathroom with an elevated ceiling and claw-footed tub occupies the second floor of the tower. A super-sized master bedroom features a compartmentalized bath and a roomy walk-in closet. Plans for detached garages for this home can be seen on pages 176 and 177.

DESIGN	M8829
BEDROOMS	3
BATHROOMS	2½
FIRST FLOOR	1,259 Sq. Ft.
SECOND FLOOR	1,181 Sq. Ft.
TOTAL	2,440 Sq. Ft.
PRICE	C2

QUEEN ANNE

George Barber's *The Cottage Souvenir #2* provided the inspiration for this faithful replica of a Victorian era home. The integral (recessed) second-floor porch is an important feature of homes of this vintage. Additionally, the pedimented entryway is a predominant characteristic of Queen Anne architecture. Within, most rooms contain large bays which contribute light and excitement. The spacious kitchen opens onto an oversized dining nook which leads into a huge utility room, ample enough for a freezer. An elegant open stairway leads to the second-floor bedrooms. The master suite is warmed by a wood-burning fireplace. Plans for detached garages for this home can be seen on pages 176 and 177.

LAUNDRY

BREAKFAST

FIRST FLOOR

DINING ROOM
12-0 x 14-6

KITCHEN

GREAT ROOM
15-0 x 18-0

UP

LIVING ROOM
12-6 x 15-6

BEDROOM
12-0 x 14-0

BEDROOM
11x0 x 11-6

BEDROOM
11-6 x 14-0

DOWN

SECOND FLOOR

MASTER
BEDROOM
12-6 x 15-6

DESIGN	M8830
BEDROOMS	4
BATHROOMS	2½
FIRST FLOOR	1,408 Sq. Ft.
SECOND FLOOR	1,194 Sq. Ft.
TOTAL	2,566 Sq. Ft.
PRICE	C2

WIDTH 38'
DEPTH 50'

LAUN

GREAT ROOM
15-6 x 17-6

BREAKFAST

LIVNG ROOM
11-6 x 15-0

KITCHEN

FIRST FLOOR

UP

DINING ROOM
11-6 x 17-6

This breathtaking Queen Anne Victorian home features a spectacular wraparound porch that culminates in an octagonal pavilion, ideal for gatherings on pleasant days. This shape is repeated in the tower that arises from the center of the house. An elongated dining room easily holds a multi-leaved table; a thoroughly up-to-date kitchen overlooks the great room. The formal living room may be converted to a guest room with only a little rearranging. Above, the master suite contains a partitioned sitting area. Its opulent bath has an unusual amount of built-in storage. All upstairs bedrooms contain walk-in closets. Plans for detached garages for this home can be seen on pages 176 and 177.

BEDROOM
12-0 x 15-6

SECOND FLOOR

BEDROOM
11-6 x 13-0

DOWN

SITTING AREA

MASTER BEDROOM
13-0 x 17-6

WIDTH 52'
DEPTH 51'

DESIGN	M8831
BEDROOMS	3
BATHROOMS	2 ½
FIRST FLOOR	1,364 Sq. Ft.
SECOND FLOOR	1,283 Sq. Ft.
TOTAL	2,647 Sq. Ft.
PRICE	C2

A wraparound porch and an octagonal tower are authentic details of this Queen Anne home. High-ceilinged rooms, with angles and bays, accurately reflect the Victorian love of unpredictability and whimsy. The expansive kitchen has a center work island; it leads into a window-encircled breakfast bay. The dining room is planned so that its beautifully arrayed table is visible from the foyer. On the second floor, two of the three hall bedrooms share a compartmentalized bath with separate vanities; the third has a private bath. The lengthy master suite has ample room for a sitting area. Its full bath features a sumptuous step-up whirlpool tub. Plans for detached garages for this home can be seen on pages 176 and 177.

FIRST FLOOR

LAUNDRY
KITCHEN
DINING ROOM
14-0 x 14-0
GREAT ROOM
14-0 x 18-0
LIVING ROOM
12-0 x 13-0
BREAKFAST
UP

SECOND FLOOR

BEDROOM
12-0 x 14-0
BEDROOM
12-0 x 14-0
BEDROOM
11-6 x 14-0
DOWN
MASTER
BEDROOM
13-0 x 18-6

DESIGN	M8832
BEDROOMS	4
BATHROOMS	3½
FIRST FLOOR	1,417 Sq. Ft.
SECOND FLOOR	1,380 Sq. Ft.
TOTAL	2,797 Sq. Ft.
PRICE	C2

WIDTH 51'
DEPTH 42'

FIRST FLOOR

GREAT ROOM
17-0 x 25-0

LAUNDRY   KITCHEN

BEDROOM
12-0 x 14-0

UP   DINING ROOM
12-0 x 14-0

SECOND FLOOR

MASTER BEDROOM
17-0 x 25-0

DOWN

BEDROOM
12-0 x 14-0

OPEN

BEDROOM
12-0 x 13-0

WIDTH 48'
DEPTH 49'

This beguiling Victorian home, with its double tier of porches, features a dramatic pair of Palladian windows. These graceful windows flood the foyer and the second-floor landing with glittering light. The foyer contains a striking stairway, angled to repeat the entryway. The first-floor bedroom can be adapted for use as a study or library if needed. The spacious kitchen has a built-in dining nook; beyond, a commodious great room opens onto a deep and shady porch. Upstairs, the master bedroom is warmed by a cheery fireplace; it opens onto a private second-floor terrace. Each bedroom in this plan has a private bath. Plans for detached garages for this home can be seen on pages 176 and 177.

DESIGN	M8833
BEDROOMS	4
BATHROOMS	4
FIRST FLOOR	1,390 Sq. Ft.
SECOND FLOOR	1,292 Sq. Ft.
TOTAL	2,682 Sq. Ft.
PRICE	C2

Doubled classical columns set on pedestals are an unusual but authentic architectural detail found in the Victorian era. Inside, an especially spacious foyer displays a traditional L-shaped stairway with an open well. The extra width in the dining room accommodates cherished heirloom furniture; just beyond, the bayed kitchen with its large island is open to a sun-filled breakfast room/gallery. A deep back porch serves as additional space for out-of-doors living. The study can also function as a guest room with its own private bath. Upstairs, the elegant master suite has ample room for a sitting area; the bath has His and Hers walk-in closets. Plans for detached garages for this home can be seen on pages 176 and 177.

FIRST FLOOR

GREAT ROOM
15-0 x 17-6

LAUN

KITCHEN

BREAKFAST

SITTING AREA

CLO

STUDY
13-0 x 16-0

UP

DINING ROOM
15-0 x 15-6

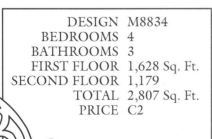

DESIGN	M8834
BEDROOMS	4
BATHROOMS	3
FIRST FLOOR	1,628 Sq. Ft.
SECOND FLOOR	1,179
TOTAL	2,807 Sq. Ft.
PRICE	C2

WIDTH 54'
DEPTH 47'

SECOND FLOOR

BEDROOM
12-0 x 13-0

DOWN

MASTER BEDROOM
15-0 x 19-6

BEDROOM
12-0 x 13-0

PORCH

L'AUNDRY

BREAKFAST

DECK

FIRST FLOOR

KITCHEN

GREAT ROOM
15-6 x 21-0

DINING ROOM
12-0 x 17-0

DN

UP

LIVING ROOM
13-0 x 16-0

SECOND FLOOR

MASTER BEDROOM
15-0 x 19-0

BATH

BEDROOM
12-0 x 15-0

DN

BATH

BEDROOM
13-0 x 14-0

WIDTH 45'
DEPTH 60'

Appreciators of the Victorian era will exult in the carefully preserved exterior details of this stunning house. A graceful veranda wraps around the charming facade, providing covered access to the foyer and to the great room. The angled foyer with repetitively shaped stairs is a popular 19th-Century feature. A super-sized dining room will accommodate a long table; the dramatically angled breakfast bay offers a second tantalizing place in which to dine. The double-tiered back porch eases the transition to the out-of-doors. Above, a master dressing suite contains two exceptional closets. The other bedrooms have a divided bath and walk-in closets. Plans for detached garages for this home can be found on pages 176 and 177.

DESIGN	M8835
BEDROOMS	3
BATHROOMS	2½
FIRST FLOOR	1,440 Sq. Ft.
SECOND FLOOR	1,358 Sq. Ft.
TOTAL	2,798 Sq. Ft.
PRICE	C2

The two-storied bay that projects from the dominant front-facing gable of this Folk Victorian adds to its charm and elegance. The transom-topped oval-glassed door opens into a long foyer with U-shaped stairs. Beyond the formal living and dining rooms, the foyer leads to a spacious great room warmed by a fireplace that is flanked with French doors. The bay-windowed breakfast nook is adjacent to the well-planned kitchen. A first-floor guest suite offers privacy and seclusion. Above, three more bedrooms and a large master suite are also zoned for privacy. The master bedroom is particularly relaxing with its separate sitting area. Plans for detached garages for this home can be seen on pages 176 and 177.

FIRST FLOOR

LAUNDRY

KITCHEN

GREAT ROOM
16-6 X 19-0

GUEST ROOM
10-6 X 13-6

BREAKFAST

LIVING ROOM
11-0 X 13-0

UP

DINING ROOM
11-6 X 13-0

SECOND FLOOR

BEDROOM
12-6 X 14-0

BEDROOM
11-0 X 13-0

DOWN

MASTER BEDROOM
13-0 X 17-0

SITTING

BEDROOM
11-6 X 13-0

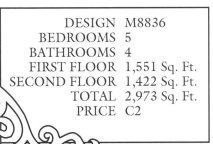

DESIGN	M8836
BEDROOMS	5
BATHROOMS	4
FIRST FLOOR	1,551 Sq. Ft.
SECOND FLOOR	1,422 Sq. Ft.
TOTAL	2,973 Sq. Ft.
PRICE	C2

WIDTH 44'
DEPTH 45'

FIRST FLOOR

GREAT ROOM
15-0 x 20-0

BREAKFAST

GUEST BEDROOM
12-6 x 15-0

KITCHEN

LAUN

UP

DINING ROOM
13-0 x 16-6

SECOND FLOOR

BEDROOM
13-6 x 14-0

MASTER BEDROOM
15-0 x 18-0

DOWN

BEDROOM
13-0 x 15-6

WIDTH 53'
DEPTH 54'

The beckoning porch of this appealing dwelling has many authentic Victorian details, such as the double-tiered front-facing pediments that crown the first- and second-floor doors. The angled side entry onto the front porch is another architectural highlight. Once inside, the spaciousness of the foyer extends an instant welcome. An extra-long dining room features a dramatic bay. Just beyond, a well-appointed kitchen is at the center of family activities. The first-floor guest suite can serve as a study or hobby room, if desired. Upstairs, two large bedrooms have walk-in closets; the capacious master suite has His and Hers vanities and His and Hers closets. Plans for detached garages for this home can be seen on pages 176 and 177.

DESIGN	M8837
BEDROOMS	4
BATHROOMS	3½
FIRST FLOOR	1,534 Sq. Ft.
SECOND FLOOR	1,448 Sq. Ft.
TOTAL	2,982 Sq. Ft.
PRICE	C2

The inspiration for this spellbinding residence came from the beloved Victorian architect, George Barber. The lacy veranda that embraces the exterior of this enchanting home offers outdoor living space under its shady recesses. Within, spacious bayed rooms create additional pizazz, as well as contributing light and floor space. The roomy kitchen is chock-full of the latest amenities, including a sit-down bar on the long work island. A supersized utility room facilitates clothes-handling chores. On the floor above, an enormous master suite has a separate shower, whirlpool tub, and plenty of dressing space. The other three bedrooms have large closets, as well. Plans for detached garages for this home can be seen on pages 176 and 177.

FIRST FLOOR

SECOND FLOOR

DESIGN	M8838
BEDROOMS	4
BATHROOMS	2½
FIRST FLOOR	1,959 Sq. Ft.
SECOND FLOOR	1,765 Sq. Ft.
TOTAL	3,724 Sq. Ft.
PRICE	C3

WIDTH 56'
DEPTH 56'

QUEEN ANNE

LAUN

BREAKFAST

KITCHEN

KEEPING ROOM
15-6 x 15-6

FIRST FLOOR

DINING ROOM
12-0 X 13-6

UP

GUEST ROOM
11-0 X12-6

GREAT ROOM
15-0 X 19-0

BEDROOM
11-0 X 13-6

BEDROOM
12-6 X 13-6

BEDROOM
12-0 X 13-6

DOWN

UP

SECOND FLOOR

MASTER
BEDROOM
15-0 X 15-0

WIDTH 44'
DEPTH 55'

The decoratively rich facade of this lively Queen Anne house indicates a passion for Victorian authenticity. An impressive entryway is topped by a porch pediment that adds extra emphasis to the facade. Within, the intriguing stairway provides an opportunity for accuracy in Victorian millwork. The kitchen, however, is full of the most modern technologic advancements. The serious cook will appreciate the walk-in food closet and the butler's pantry that leads into the dining room. There is a first-floor guest suite; above, four other bedrooms easily accommodate the larger family. The master bedroom is the proud possessor of an elaborate bath located in the high-ceilinged tower. Plans for detached garages for this home can be seen on pages 176 and 177.

DESIGN	M8839
BEDROOMS	5
BATHROOMS	4
FIRST FLOOR	1,578 Sq. Ft.
SECOND FLOOR	1,418 Sq. Ft.
TOTAL	2,996 Sq. Ft.
PRICE	C2

FOLK VICTORIAN

This sparkling Victorian is encircled by a graceful porch with turned columns resting on elevated pedestals. A second-story porch creates additional interest and repeats the doubled columns below. Within, a resplendent foyer looks into an expansive great room and beyond to a spacious dining room. The enormous kitchen houses a second set of stairs to facilitate the flow of family traffic. The glass-encircled living room is zoned well away from the uproar of family life. On the second floor, four bedrooms have been planned. The master suite is particularly inviting, with its opulent bath and separate closets. The kitchen stairs originate conveniently near the back bedrooms. Plans for detached garages for this home can be seen on pages 176 and 177.

DESIGN	M8840
BEDROOMS	4
BATHROOMS	3½
FIRST FLOOR	1,834 Sq. Ft.
SECOND FLOOR	1,664 Sq. Ft.
TOTAL	3,498 Sq. Ft.
PRICE	C3

FIRST FLOOR

SECOND FLOOR

WIDTH 62'
DEPTH 52'

GARAGE
24-0 x 24-0

FIRST FLOOR

BREAKFAST

KITCHEN

GREAT ROOM
15-0 x 26-0

UP

DINING ROOM
13-6 x 17-6

LIVING ROOM
13-0 x 16-0

STORAGE

BEDROOM
11-6 x 19-0

MASTER BEDROOM
15-0 x 21-0

LAUNDRY

UP

DOWN

SECOND FLOOR

BEDROOM
12-0 x 13-6

BEDROOM
13-0 x 14-0

WIDTH 48'
DEPTH 68'

The Italianate heritage of this imposing Victorian design is revealed in
such architectural elements as the
centered squared tower, the long
narrow windows, and its three-storied
appearance. The updated floor plan
remains very close to the original
house. Formal living and dining
rooms are warmed by wood-burning
fireplaces. Beyond, an expansive great
room is tucked away near the kitchen
and breakfast area. On the second
floor, a majestic three-storied tower
floods the second-floor hallway with
light. An additional stairway can be
constructed to the third floor and a
high-ceilinged tower room finished.
The four large bedrooms that occupy
the rest of the second floor include a
sumptuous master suite with elaborate closets and a compartmentalized
dressing area.

DESIGN	M8841
BEDROOMS	4
BATHROOMS	3½
FIRST FLOOR	1,582 Sq. Ft.
SECOND FLOOR	1,854 Sq. Ft.
TOTAL	3,436 Sq. Ft.
PRICE	C3

FOLK-TYPE FARMHOUSE

The first-floor guest bedroom in this charming residence lends great flexibility to the plan. If required, this room could function as a secluded study, hobby room, or a home office. An exceptionally generous breakfast bay provides ample room for family dining. The stairs rise conveniently from the great room, and lead to a spacious second-floor landing, well-lit by a Palladian window. The master suite houses a luxurious bath, with a corner tub and an angled shower. Both upstairs bedrooms feature oversized closets with ample room for clothes. Plans for detached garages for this home can be seen on pages 176 and 177.

GREAT ROOM
13-6 x 18-6

BREAKFAST

FIRST FLOOR

UP

KITCHEN

LAUN

DINING ROOM
11-0 x 12-0

GUEST BEDROOM
11-6 x 12-0

SECOND FLOOR

MASTER BEDROOM
11-6 x 12-6

DOWN

BEDROOM
10-0 x 11-0

DESIGN	M8842
BEDROOMS	3
BATHROOMS	3½
FIRST FLOOR	1,093 Sq. Ft.
SECOND FLOOR	628 Sq. Ft.
TOTAL	1,721 Sq. Ft.
PRICE	C1

WIDTH 32'
DEPTH 39'

FIRST FLOOR

LAUNDRY

BREAKFAST

KITCHEN

DINING ROOM
13·0 x 11·6

UP

GREAT ROOM
13·0 x 18·0

SECOND FLOOR

BEDROOM
11·6 x 14·0

BEDROOM
11·6 x 12·0

DOWN

MASTER
BEDROOM
14·0 x 14·0

WIDTH 32'
DEPTH 40'

The quaint and restful appeal of this peaceful Farmhouse design will make it suitable for either an urban or a rural setting. The openness of this plan lends the impression of a house much larger than its square footage reveals. The floor plan, with its careful attention to circulation, makes the house especially adaptable to entertaining. Ascending conveniently from the center of the house, the stairway is illuminated by two windows. The second-floor bedrooms are particularly spacious; the master includes two separate closets, as well as a compartmentalized bath and a whirlpool tub. Plans for detached garages for this home can be seen on pages 176 and 177.

DESIGN	M8843
BEDROOMS	3
BATHROOMS	2½
FIRST FLOOR	928 Sq. Ft.
SECOND FLOOR	875 Sq. Ft.
TOTAL	1,803 Sq. Ft.
PRICE	C1

RUSTIC FARMHOUSE

GUEST BEDROOM
11-0 x 13-0

FIRST FLOOR

BREAKFAST

GREAT ROOM
16-0 x 19-0

PANTRY

KITCHEN

UP

DINING ROOM
14-0 x 17-0

BEDROOM
13-0 x 14-0

DOWN

SECOND FLOOR

BEDROOM
13-0 x 15-0

MASTER BEDROOM
14-0 x 17-0

The 1868 edition of *Bicknell's Victorian Buildings* provided the inspiration for this classic home. The multiple bays that project from its clean and simple lines add architectural pizazz to the exterior and provide sunlit living spaces on the interior. An oversized dining room, ideal for displaying cherished antiques, opens off the foyer. Opposite this room, a commodious great room is warmed by a wood-burning fireplace. The first-floor guest suite can double as a secluded study. Upstairs, three oversized bedrooms possess an unusual amount of closet space; the master suite contains two separate closets. Plans for detached garages for this home can be seen on pages 176 and 177.

DESIGN	M8844
BEDROOMS	4
BATHROOMS	3
FIRST FLOOR	1,178 Sq. Ft.
SECOND FLOOR	1,078 Sq. Ft.
TOTAL	2,256 Sq. Ft.
PRICE	C2

WIDTH 42'
DEPTH 48'

FIRST FLOOR

LAUN

BREAKFAST

UP

KITCHEN

GREAT ROOM
19-6 x 20-0

DINING ROOM
13-6 x 14-6

SECOND FLOOR

BEDROOM
12-0 x 13-6

MASTER
BEDROOM
13-6 x 19-6

DOWN

BEDROOM
12-0 x 13-6

WIDTH 43'
DEPTH 45'

Board-and-batten siding, floor-to-ceiling windows, and a simplified porch railing contribute to the overall relaxed feeling of this French-style Farmhouse. Its familiar T-shape lends itself to natural ventilation and is a classic where seasons are moderate. Stairs that rise in the kitchen mean added convenience for a family on the go. The large walk-in closet provides ample storage for food supplies and serving pieces. An L-shaped rear porch is easily accessed from both the great room and the breakfast area. Above, a second-floor porch opens off the master suite and the back bedroom. Bedrooms feature a partitioned bath and walk-in closets. Plans for detached garages for this home can be seen on pages 176 and 177.

DESIGN	M8845
BEDROOMS	3
BATHROOMS	2½
FIRST FLOOR	1,190 Sq. Ft.
SECOND FLOOR	1,102 Sq. Ft.
TOTAL	2,292 Sq. Ft.
PRICE	C2

This Farmhouse design, with its long and welcoming porch, is a classic design that will never go out of style. An unusual floor plan, that isolates formal areas from family living, offers generously proportioned rooms perfect for displaying cherished antiques. The kitchen features a work island and a walk-in pantry for food storage; the butler's pantry that connects the kitchen and dining room is an ideal location for a wet bar. A rear staircase facilitates access to the bedrooms above. Here, three bedrooms are planned with a fourth room that can serve as a study or nursery. An unusually large amount of closet space is provided for those with storage needs. Plans for detached garages for this home can be found on pages 176 and 177.

FIRST FLOOR

LAUN

KITCHEN

BUTLER'S PANTRY

BREAKFAST

PAN

UP

DINING ROOM
12-6 x 14-0

GREAT ROOM
17-6 x 20-0

LIVING ROOM
12-6 x 12-6

SECOND FLOOR

BEDROOM
11-6 x 12-0

BEDROOM
11-6 x 12-0

DOWN

BATH

BATH

MASTER BEDROOM
14-0 x 16-6

STUDY
9-0 x 11-0

DESIGN	M8846
BEDROOMS	3
BATHROOMS	2½
FIRST FLOOR	1,332 Sq. Ft.
SECOND FLOOR	1,271 Sq. Ft.
TOTAL	2,595 Sq. Ft.
PRICE	C2

WIDTH 37'
DEPTH 48'

FIRST FLOOR

BREAKFAST

KITCHEN

LAUN

GREAT ROOM
15-0 x 15-0

DINING ROOM
12-0 x 15-0

UP

LIVING ROOM
12-0 x 15-0

SECOND FLOOR

BEDROOM
10-6 x 12-6

BATH

MASTER
BEDROOM
11-0 x 16-6

DOWN

BEDROOM
10-6 x 12-6

BEDROOM
10-6 x 12-6

OPEN TO
BELOW

WIDTH 44'

DEPTH 49'

The front-facing gable that projects from the center of this inviting dwelling is highlighted by a glittering Palladian window. The magnificent foyer is open all the way to the ceiling of the second floor; this same Palladian contributes sunlight to both the first and second stories. In this very old-fashioned formal plan, a living room and dining room open onto separate front porches. Modern advancements, however, are apparent in the roomy country kitchen and bayed breakfast room. An oversized walk-in pantry is ample enough to contain a freezer, if desired. Above, the master suite reflects the bay below in a dazzling bathroom arrangement. Plans for detached garages for this home can be seen on pages 176 and 177.

DESIGN	M8847
BEDROOMS	4
BATHROOMS	2½
FIRST FLOOR	1,430 Sq. Ft.
SECOND FLOOR	1,160 Sq. Ft.
TOTAL	2,590 Sq. Ft.
PRICE	C2

The front-facing gable of this classic Farmhouse accentuates the authentic transom-topped doorway below. The long front porch provides additional living space on temperate days. An exceptionally wide foyer instantly imparts an aura of spaciousness. The convenient walk-through bar connects the living room to the great room and facilitates entertaining. A spacious kitchen features a sizable walk-in pantry and a built-in desk. The handy laundry room has space for an upright freezer. Above, three bedrooms and the master suite are isolated from the noise of family living. The master bath, partitioned for comfort and privacy, has separate His and Hers closets. Plans for detached garages for this home can be seen on pages 176 and 177.

FIRST FLOOR

BREAKFAST
LAUNDRY
GREAT ROOM
16-0 x 19-0
KITCHEN
PANTRY
BAR
DINING ROOM
12-0 x 13-0
LIVING ROOM
12-0 x 13-0
UP

SECOND FLOOR

BEDROOM
11-6 x 12-6
BEDROOM
11-6 x 13-0
DOWN
MASTER BEDROOM
13-0 x 18-6
BEDROOM
12-0 x 13-0

DESIGN	M8848
BEDROOMS	4
BATHROOMS	3½
FIRST FLOOR	1,368 Sq. Ft.
SECOND FLOOR	1,280 Sq. Ft.
TOTAL	2,648 Sq. Ft.
PRICE	C2

WIDTH 40'
DEPTH 36'

GUEST
11-6 X 12-0

GREAT ROOM
14-6 X 19-0

BREAKFAST

KITCHEN

UP

LIVING ROOM
12-6 X 14-6

DINING ROOM
11-6 X 13-0

FIRST FLOOR

The irresistible appeal of this pleasing dwelling is due in part to its wide front porch. Additional enchantment emanates from the front-facing gable with its characteristic ornamentation. Inside, a centrally located stairway is an assist to family traffic patterns. The dining and kitchen wings open onto both formal and informal living areas to provide easy circulation. A private first-floor guest suite is isolated well away from other bedroom areas. Upstairs, the luxurious master suite has a wood-burning fireplace. The adjacent built-in can accommodate television or stereo equipment as well as books for bedtime reading. Two hall bedrooms share a compartmentalized bath. Plans for detached garages for this home can be seen on pages 176 and 177.

MASTER BEDROOM
14-6 X 19-0

LAUN

DOWN

BEDROOM
11-6 X 12-0

BEDROOM
12-0 X 12-6

SECOND FLOOR

WIDTH 44'
DEPTH 48'

DESIGN	M8849
BEDROOMS	4
BATHROOMS	3
FIRST FLOOR	1,462 Sq. Ft.
SECOND FLOOR	1,112 Sq. Ft.
TOTAL	2,574 Sq. Ft.
PRICE	C2

CLASSIC FARMHOUSE

The tantalizing porch of this classic Farmhouse design imparts charm and warmth to this impressive residence. An exceptionally wide entrance foyer, flanked by a living room and dining room, contributes to the aura of spaciousness and welcome. The roomy country kitchen with its long expanse of counter space is adjoined by a spacious utility room. Past the commodious great room, a secluded guest suite offers lucky visitors privacy and quiet. On the second floor, an expansive master suite contains two very large closets. Each of the hall bedrooms has its own private bath and walk-in closet. Plans for detached garages for this home can be seen on pages 176 and 177.

BREAKFAST

KITCHEN

GREAT ROOM
16-6 x 21-0

GUEST
ROOM
10-6 x 14-0

FIRST FLOOR

LAUNDRY

UP

DINING ROOM
12-6 x 14-6

LIVING ROOM
12-6 x 14-6

SKYLIGHT

MASTER BEDROOM
16-6 x 21-0

SECOND FLOOR

DOWN

BEDROOM
12-6 x 14-6

BEDROOM
12-6 x 14-6

DESIGN	M8850
BEDROOMS	4
BATHROOMS	4½
FIRST FLOOR	1,884 Sq. Ft.
SECOND FLOOR	1,340 Sq. Ft.
TOTAL	3,224 Sq. Ft.
PRICE	C3

WIDTH 62'
DEPTH 46'

FIRST FLOOR

KITCHEN   BREAKFAST
GREAT ROOM
17-6 x 20-6

LAUNDRY

LAU. CHUTE

DINING ROOM
14-0 x 18-0

MASTER BEDROOM
16-6 x 18-6

LIVING ROOM
16-6 x 22-0

UP

STUDY
12-6 x 16-6

The transom-topped entryway, crowned with a pedimented gable with graceful detailing, welcomes family and friends to this home. Within, a formal living and dining room, each with its own bay, reflect the original floor plan layout of this authentic replica. Across the wide hall, the master suite features a private study and sumptuous bath. The roomy country kitchen has a work island, a built-in desk, and adjoins an informal dining area and the great room. An old-fashioned butler's pantry connects the kitchen to the dining room. Above, four bedrooms share the two compartmentalized baths. Plans for detached garages for this home can be seen on pages 176 and 177.

SECOND FLOOR

BEDROOM
14-0 x 14-0

DOWN

BEDROOM
12-0 x 16-6

BEDROOM
13-6 x 16-6

BEDROOM
12-0 x 16-6

DESIGN	M8851
BEDROOMS	5
BATHROOMS	3½
FIRST FLOOR	2,872 Sq. Ft.
SECOND FLOOR	1,600 Sq. Ft.
TOTAL	4,472 Sq. Ft.
PRICE	C4

WIDTH 60'
DEPTH 70'

This well-designed, detached garage plan beautifully complements any of the Victorian or Farmhouse designs shown on pages 124-175. Beneath its quaint hip roof is an area large enough for two cars. Attached is a giant area for garden tools, hobby or play equipment and other hard-to-store items. Choose the two-car option (M8852) or the three-car option (M8853).

STORAGE

GARAGE
22-0 x 24-0

M8852—TWO-CAR GARAGE

DESIGN	M8852
SQUARE FOOTAGE	750
PRICE	C5

DESIGN	M8853
SQUARE FOOTAGE	782
PRICE	C6

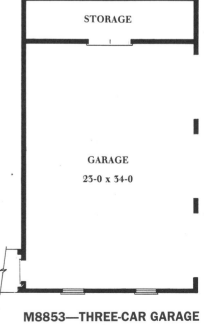

STORAGE

GARAGE
23-0 x 34-0

M8853—THREE-CAR GARAGE

FIRST FLOOR

STORAGE

UP

GARAGE
22-0 x 24-0

SECOND FLOOR

DOWN

BONUS ROOM
15-0 x 22-0

M8854—TWO-CAR GARAGE

Here's an authentically styled, detached garage with an added attraction—a bonus room upstairs! This gable-roofed plan fits well with any of the Victorian or Farmhouse designs shown on pages 124-175. Besides room for the family autos, there's storage space accessed from outside. Choose the two-car option (M8854) or the three-car option (M8855).

STORAGE

UP

GARAGE
23-0 x 34-0

FIRST FLOOR

DOWN

BONUS ROOM
13-6 x 34-0

SECOND FLOOR

M8855—THREE-CAR GARAGE

DESIGN	M8854
GARAGE	750 Sq. Ft.
BONUS ROOM	425 Sq. Ft.
TOTAL	1,175 Sq. Ft.
PRICE	C5

DESIGN	M8855
GARAGE	1,050 Sq. Ft.
BONUS ROOM	575 Sq. Ft.
TOTAL	1,625 Sq. Ft.
PRICE	C6

HISTORICAL REPLICATIONS, INC.

INCLUDED IN YOUR BLUEPRINTS ARE:

A Foundation Plan with a conventional crawl-space foundation layout including all necessary notations and dimensions. When an attached garage is part of the design, its concrete slab foundation and details are included also.

Fully Detailed Floor Plans reflecting all dimensions necessary for accurate framing and detailed layout and location of all electrical components and plumbing fixtures.

Exterior Elevations, which are views of the front, rear, right and left sides of your home. The finish materials and overall proportions and design are shown in these elevations.

Interior Elevations, which are interior views showing all kitchen, bath, fireplace, powder room, special built-ins and cabinet designs for your particular home.

A Complete Window And Door Schedule with sizes and styles recommended for the windows and doors included in the house design you select.

Building Cross Sections, cornice sections, fireplace sections and cabinet sections necessary to assist the builder in visualizing and understanding complicated interior details of major components of the home.

Framing Diagrams that show layouts of framing components and their locations for roof, first floor and second floor. This is especially important when a design consists of complex and unusual structural elements.

Energy Saving Details which specify such proven features as vapor barriers, insulated sheathing, caulking, foam sealant, batt insulation, wood windows and attic exhaust ventilators—in order to obtain R-19 in the walls and R-38 in the ceiling.

Typical Details And Sections displaying both interior and exterior techniques recommended in the completion of the design you have selected.

Note: All plans have been drawn to conform to basic FHA and VA regulations. Since the local codes for your area could vary slightly, modifications may be necessary to meet regional requirements.

Foundation Note: All of our plans are designed for a crawl-space foundation. Many of our designs can be readily adapted to a basement plan. An experienced builder can usually accomplish this alteration without our involvement; however, if interior or exterior design modifications are required, please contact a member of our staff for an estimate of our fee for this modification.

Some of our customers wish to build our houses on concrete slab foundations. In this sitation, the interior floor plan must be slightly rearranged to allow for an HVAC closet and ductwork. Again, please call or write our offices for a quote on this type of alteration.

Mechanical Note: Heating and air conditioning layouts are not included in our plans. Your local mechanical contractor will size and locate the proper unit for your particular climatic conditions.

PRICE SCHEDULE

	C1	C2	C3	C4
One-set package	$250	$300	$375	$450
Five-set package	$295	$345	$420	$495
Eight-set package	$330	$380	$455	$530

Additional sets of working drawings $15
Mirror-reverse (dimensions & lettering will read backward) $25

	C5	C6
Garage Plans:	2-Car Garage	3-Car Garage
One-set package	$50	$60
Five-set package	$85	$95
Eight-set package	$110	$120

Additional sets of garage working drawings $10

TO ORDER BLUEPRINTS, TURN TO PAGE 187.

For more information on these plans, write:
Historical Replications, Inc., P.O. Box 13529, Jackson, Mississippi 39236

GREAT OUTDOOR PROJECTS

No house should go empty-landed for long. If you're searching for just the right structure to fill up those wide open spaces, we've got some solid choices to show you. Among these exciting plans you'll find a get-away-from-it-all gazebo that's big enough for small gatherings; a storage shed that does a number on clutter but looks great doing it; a two-dormer studio garage with all the comforts of home and a nice old-timey feel; and a gorgeous little crafts cottage with one very bright touch: an attached sunroom.

OUTDOOR PROJECTS INDEX & PRICE SCHEDULE

TO ORDER, CALL TOLL FREE 1-800-848-2550, OR SEE PAGE 187.

Our gazebo is a prime spot for entertaining. At 200-plus square feet of decking, it has as much surface space as the average family room. Plus, it's just under 17½ feet tall, which makes it the size of a typical one-story house. As a result, it's best suited for larger lots—at least a half acre. Boasting a number of neo-classic features—perfect proportions, columns, bases—it's also a good match with Victorians and Farmhouses. The cupola is a homey touch that lets light in to the decking below. Cedar or redwood are the building materials of choice.

DESIGN MG108

WIDTH 12'
DEPTH 12'

SUNROOM

DECK

WORK TABLE

UP

Great space for a cottage industry, this little building (250 square feet) is both functional and good looking. Ample counter space and shelving provide plenty of room to spread out materials and tools. Plus, a vaulted ceiling opens up the whole area. Next to the work space is a cozy sunroom (vaulted ceiling here, too). French doors and several windows, including a circle-head version above the doors, bathe the room in sunlight, while overhangs offer adequate shading. To get maximum sun, a south facing for the sunroom is best; it will also provide soft, even illumination for the north-facing work area.

DESIGN MG109

WIDTH 20'
DEPTH 16'

INTERIOR VIEW

Imagine this charming structure perched adjacent to your backyard swimming pool. Its exterior high-lights such architectural features as hip and gable roofs, a decorative cupola, shuttered windows, flower boxes, and horizontal wood and shingle siding. Its plan offers a spacious sheltered party/lounge area with counter, sink and refrigerator space. An optional built-in table could assure no rain-outs of pool-side dining. Flanking this practical breeze-way-type area are two rooms equal in size and utility. To the left is the changing room with a convenient bench. To the right is the equipment room for the handy storage of pool supplies and furniture. Surely a fine addition to the active family's back-yard.

WIDTH 24'
DEPTH 12' 8"

DESIGN MG110

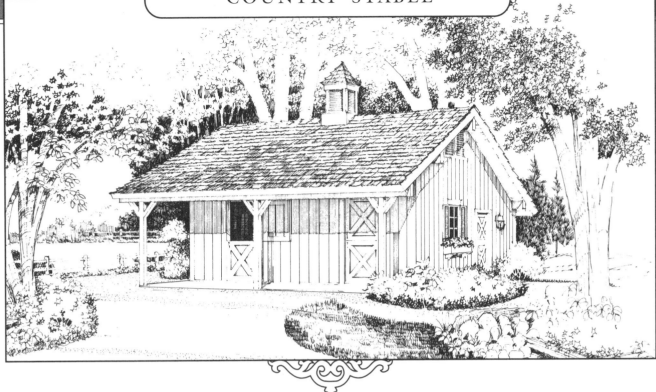

WIDTH 24'
DEPTH 24'
DEPTH WITH COVERED PORCH 32'

HAY STORAGE
$14^2 \times 7^0$

TACK/FEED
$8^8 \times 7^0$

TACKING / GROOMING

STALL
$11^6 \times 9^2$

STALL
$11^6 \times 9^2$

COVERED PORCH

Charming, cross-hatched Dutch doors and a steepled roof are fitting country touches for this free-standing stable. Two horses and all their gear share plenty of room in two stalls, a tack and feed room, and a hay storage area. A long central corridor, with one wide and one regular entrance, contributes space for grooming your favorite mount or saddling up for a morning ride. The covered porch on the stall side acts as a weather buffer, keeping rain and hot sun away from precious animals. Shuttered windows are accented with window boxes. No horses? With some simple modifications, the stable becomes a writer's cottage or gardening workshop.

DESIGN MG113

STORAGE SHED WITH PATIO

Here's a hard-working storage shed with a number of bright touches. At 120 square feet, it's bigger than most. Cupola, birdhouse, shutters, and grooved plywood siding add up to a traditional look that complements many popular housing styles—from Victorians to Farmhouses. It's a flexible design, too, and could also be a potting shed, lath-house or work-shop. The nicest feature may well be the covered patio. After you cut the grass, just stash the lawn mower, take a seat and survey your handiwork.

DESIGN MG107

WIDTH 12'
DEPTH 12'

COVERED PATIO
10⁰ x 10⁰

STORAGE AREA

WORKBENCH

STUDIO
23⁴ x 13² +DORMERS

BOOK SHELVES   BATH LINEN   BOOK SHELVES

ROOF

RAILING

DN.

ROOF

GARAGE
23⁴ x 23⁴

W.H. FURN.

P.

WIDTH 24'
DEPTH 24'

UP

Can you top this? Our two-car garage has an artist's studio nestled snugly on the second floor. The Cape Cod-style design, with three dormers, large shutters, paneled doors and characteristic proportions of roof to floor, makes a strong visual statement that would complement a large number of traditional housing styles. An exterior staircase, covered at the top, leads to 300 square feet of fully insulated studio space; adjacent is a full 4x7-foot bath with shower and linen storage.

DESIGN MG106

PLAN AND PRICE INDEX

LARRY W. GARNETT & ASSOCIATES

PLAN	SCHEDULE	PAGE
M9000	A5	59
M9001	A4	57
M9002	A2	58
M9003	A4	56
M9004	A5	60
M9005	A5	61
M9006	A1	54
M9007	A1	53
M9008	A4	14
M9009	A4	20
M9010	A4	28
M9011	A4	29
M9012	A4	26
M9013	A5	41
M9014	A5	33
M9015	A5	47
M9016	A5	42
M9017	A5	39
M9030	A4	15
M9032	A1	48
M9033	A1	49
M9035	A1	50
M9038	A1	52
M9039	A1	51
M9049	A4	10
M9050	A1	12
M9051	A4	11
M9052	A4	13
M9053	A4	16
M9054	A1	17
M9055	A5	18
M9056	A4	19
M9057	A5	22
M9058	A4	23
M9059	A2	24
M9060	A2	25
M9061	A3	30
M9062	A5	31
M9063	A4	32
M9064	A3	34
M9065	A3	35
M9066	A4	36
M9067	A4	37
M9068	A2	38
M9069	A5	40
M9070	A6	43
M9071	A5	44
M9072	A3	45
M9073	A5	46
M9074	A1	55
M9075	A5	62
M9076	A3	63

Price Schedules:

	A1	A2	A3	A4	A5
One-set pkg.	$185	$225	$250	$295	$325

Each additional set of same plan $25
Reversed set of same plan $25

	A6
One-set pkg.	$425

Each additional set of same plan $30
Reversed set of same plan $30

OUTDOOR PROJECTS

PLAN	PRICE	PAGE
G106	$40	185
G107	$30	184
G108	$20	180
G109	$30	181
G110	$30	182
G113	$30	183

HOME PLANNERS

PLAN	SCHEDULE	PAGE
M1354	B1	104
M1956	B1	105
M2500	B2	102
M2527	B3	103
M2565	B2	100
M2597	B2	101
M2645	B3	85
M2646	B2	96
M2647	B4	97
M2650	B2	115
M2664	B2	113
M2681	B2	109
M2694	B3	112
M2774	B2	111
M2776	B2	116
M2786	B2	106
M2829	B4	99
M2865	B3	117
M2874	B4	98
M2890	B3	114
M2908	B2	107
M2945	B2	108
M2946	B3	110
M2953	B5	95
M2954	B5	94
M2969	B3	84
M2970	B4	90
M2971	B3	82
M2972	B2	80
M2973	B2	76
M2974	B1	67
M3304	B5	92
M3307	B3	81
M3308	B5	93
M3309	B2	77
M3382	B3	74
M3383	B3	66
M3384	B3	73
M3385	B3	68
M3386	B5	87
M3387	B5	89
M3388	B4	79
M3389	B3	70
M3390	B3	69
M3391	B3	71
M3392	B4	88
M3393	B3	72
M3394	B4	78
M3395	B5	86
M3396	B3	118
M3397	B4	120
M3398	B3	121
M3399	B4	119

Price Schedules:

	B1	B2	B3	B4	B5
One-set pkg.	$180	$210	$240	$270	$360
Four-set pkg.	$240	$270	$300	$330	$420
Eight-set pkg.	$300	$330	$360	$390	$480
One set of Reproducible Sepias	$360	$420	$480	$540	$600

Additional Identical Blueprints
in same order .... $40 per set
Reverse Blueprints
(Mirror Image) .... $40 per set
Specification Outlines .... $5 each
Materials Lists
Schedule B1-B4 .... $35 each
Schedule B5 .... $40 each
Additional Materials Lists
in same order .... $10 each

HISTORICAL REPLICATIONS

PLAN	SCHEDULE	PAGE
M8800	C1	124
M8801	C1	125
M8802	C1	126
M8803	C1	130
M8804	C1	128
M8805	C2	138
M8806	C1	127
M8807	C1	143
M8808	C1	132
M8809	C1	133
M8810	C1	131
M8811	C1	129
M8812	C2	134
M8813	C1	135
M8814	C1	136
M8815	C2	137
M8816	C2	140
M8817	C2	141
M8818	C1	144
M8819	C2	145
M8820	C2	139
M8821	C2	148
M8822	C2	146
M8823	C2	142
M8824	C2	150
M8825	C2	151
M8826	C2	147
M8827	C2	149
M8828	C2	152
M8829	C2	153
M8830	C2	154
M8831	C2	155
M8832	C2	156
M8833	C2	157
M8834	C2	158
M8835	C2	159
M8836	C2	160
M8837	C2	161
M8838	C3	162
M8839	C2	163
M8840	C3	164
M8841	C3	165
M8842	C1	166
M8843	C1	167
M8844	C2	168
M8845	C2	169
M8846	C2	170
M8847	C2	171
M8848	C2	172
M8849	C2	173
M8850	C3	174
M8851	C4	175
M8852	C5	176
M8853	C6	176
M8854	C5	177
M8855	C6	177

Price Schedules:

	C1	C2	C3	C4
One-set pkg	$250	$300	$375	$450
Five-set pkg.	$295	$345	$420	$495
Eight-set pkg.	$330	$380	$455	$530

Additional sets of working drawings $15
Mirror Reverse (dimensions and lettering
will read backward) $25

	C5	C6
Garage Plans:	2-Car Garage	3-Car Garage
One-set pkg.	$50	$60
Five-set pkg.	$85	$95
Eight-set pkg.	$110	$120

Additional sets of garage
working drawings $10

TO ORDER

TO ORDER

To order blueprints from any designer in this book, simply fill out the order coupon at right and mail with your remittance. If you prefer, you can also use a credit card or order C.O.D. (Sorry, no C.O.D. shipments to foreign countries, including Canada.) If time is of the essence, call our toll-free number, 1-800-848-2550.

OUR SERVICE POLICY

Upon receipt of the order coupon, we will process your order and forward it to the designer supplying the blueprints. Orders for Home Planners blueprints will be shipped within 3 days of receipt. Please allow an additional 10 days for shipment of blueprints from other designers.

NO RETURN POLICY

Because the designers in this book produce and ship plans in response to individual orders, we are not able to honor requests for refunds. Therefore, all plans are sold on a non-returnable basis.

REVERSE BLUEPRINTS

If you want to build in reverse of the plan as shown, all designers will honor your request for an extra set of reversed blueprints. Although letters and dimensions will appear backward, reverses will prove to be a useful visual aid if you decide to flop the plan. To order one set of reverse blueprints, simply mark the appropriate space in the coupon. See the index at left for the cost of each designer's reversed blueprint sets.

MODIFYING THE PLANS

Slight revisions are easy to do before you start building. Simply consult your builder or local architect to make minor alterations. If you're thinking about major changes, you will need to consult an experienced architect, engineer, or designer. You might want to purchase one set of blueprints or a set of reproducible sepias and have the plan redrawn locally. Some of the designers in this book provide alterations or custom designs to your specifications. Please consult the Blueprint Package page for each plan company to determine the services offered and then contact the designer directly.

HOW MANY BLUEPRINTS DO YOU NEED?

A single set of blueprints is sufficient to study a home in greater detail. However, if you are planning to obtain cost estimates from a contractor or subcontractors—or if you are planning to build immediately—you will need more sets. Because additional sets are usually cheaper when ordered in quantity with the original order, make sure you order enough blueprints to satisfy all requirements. The following checklist will help you determine how many you need:

_____ Owner
_____ Builder (generally requires at least three sets; one as a legal document, one to use during inspections, and at least one to give to subcontractors)
_____ Local Building Department (often requires two sets)
_____ Mortgage Lender (usually one set for a conventional loan; three sets for FHA or VA loans)
_____ TOTAL NUMBER OF SETS

TO ORDER BLUEPRINTS BY PHONE

Call toll free: 1-800-848-2550. When you order by phone, we'll ask for the Order Form Key. It's located in the lower right-hand corner of the order form on this page. Or, copy the Order Form at right and send it on our International FAX line: 1-602-297-6219.

CANADIAN CUSTOMERS

For faster, more economical service, Canadian customers may now call in orders on our Toll-Free line. Or, complete the Order Form at right, and mail with your check indicating U.S. funds to: Home Planners, Inc., 3275 W. Ina Road, Suite 110, Tucson, AZ 85741.

Order Toll Free
1-800-848-2550

 HOME PLANNERS, INC.
3275 W. INA ROAD, SUITE 110
TUCSON, AZ 85741

BASIC BLUEPRINT PACKAGE—ALL DESIGNERS

Rush me the following (please refer to the Plan and Price Index opposite):

____ Set(s) of blueprints for plan number _____ $ _____

____ Set(s) of reproducible sepias for plan number _____ $ _____

____ Set(s) of additional identical blueprints in same order $ _____

____ Set(s) of reverse blueprints $ _____

____ Set(s) of Historical Relpications garage plan number _____ $ _____

EXTRAS FOR HOME PLANNERS' PLANS ONLY

____ Materials Lists @ $35.00 first set Schedule B1–B4; $45.00 first set Schedule B5; Additional sets $10.00 each $ _____

IMPORTANT EXTRAS FOR USE WITH ANY PLAN

(see Extra Products section, pages 188–189, for details)

____ Specification Outlines @ $5.00 each $ _____

____ Detail Sets @ $14.95 each; any two for $22.95; all three for $29.95 $ _____

☐ Plumbing ☐ Electrical ☐ Construction
(These helpful details provide general construction advice and are not specific to any single plan.) $ _____

____ Plan-A-Home® @ $29.95 each $ _____

____ Set(s) of blueprints for Outdoor Project number(s)_____ $ _____

SUB-TOTAL $ _____

SALES TAX (Arizona residents add 5% sales tax; Michigan residents add 4% sales tax.) $ _____

POSTAGE AND HANDLING	1-3 sets	4 or more sets	
UPS DELIVERY (Requires street address—No P.O.Boxes)			
• UPS Regular Service Allow 4-5 days delivery	$ 6.00	$ 8.00	$ ____
• UPS 2nd Day Air Allow 2-3 days delivery	$12.00	$20.00	$ ____
• UPS Next Day Air Allow 1-2 days delivery	$22.00	$30.00	$ ____
POST OFFICE DELIVERY If no street address available. Allow 4-5 days delivery	$ 8.00	$12.00	$ ____
OVERSEAS AIR MAIL DELIVERY	$30.00	$50.00	$ ____
Note: All delivery times are from date Blueprint Package is shipped.	☐ Send C.O.D.		

TOTAL (Sub-total, tax, and postage) $ _____

YOUR ADDRESS (Please Print)

Name _____

Street _____

City _____ State _____ Zip _____

Daytime telephone number _____

FOR CREDIT CARD ORDERS ONLY ☐ MasterCard
Please fill in the information below: ☐ Visa ☐ Discover

Credit Card Number   Exp. Month/Year _____/____

_____
Signature   Order Form Key TB21BP

Important Extras To Do The Job Right!

Introducing six important planning and construction aids developed by our professionals to help you succeed in your home-building project.

To Order, Call Toll Free 1-800-848-2550

To add these important extras to your Blueprint Package, simply indicate your choices on the order form on page 187 — or call us Toll Free 1-800-848-2550 and we'll tell you more about these exciting products.

MATERIALS LIST

For many of the designs in this book, we offer a customized materials take-off that is invaluable in planning and estimating the cost of your new home. This comprehensive list outlines the quantity, type and size of material needed to build your house (with the exception of mechanical system items). Included are:

- framing lumber
- roofing and sheet metal
- windows and doors
- exterior sheathing material and trim
- masonry, veneer and fireplace materials
- tile and flooring materials
- kitchen and bath cabinetry
- interior sheathing and trim
- rough and finish hardware
- many more items

(Note: Because of differing local codes, building methods, and availability of materials, our Materials Lists do not include mechanical materials. To obtain necessary take-offs and recommendations, consult heating, plumbing and electrical contractors. Materials Lists are not sold separately from the Blueprint Package.)

This handy list helps you or your builder cost out materials and serves as a ready reference sheet when you're compiling bids. It also provides a cross-check against the materials specified by your builder and helps coordinate the substitution of items you may need to meet local codes.

SPECIFICATION OUTLINE

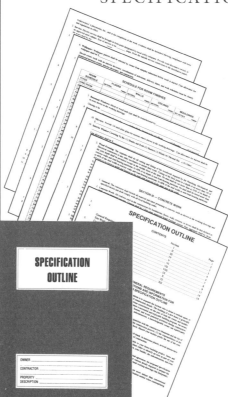

This valuable 16-page document is critical to building your house correctly. Designed to be filled in by you or your builder, this booklet lists 166 stages or items crucial to the building process.

For the layman, it provides a comprehensive review of the construction process and helps in making the specific choices of materials, models and processes. For the builder, it serves as a guide to preparing a building quotation and forms the basis for the construction program.

Designed primarily as a reference for the homeowner, this Specification Outline can become a legally binding document. Once it is filled out and agreed upon by owner and builder, it becomes a complete Project Specification.

When combined with the blueprints, a signed contract and schedule, the Specification Outline becomes a legal document and record for the building of your home. Many home builders find it useful to order two of these outlines—one as a worksheet in formulating the specifications and another to be carefully completed as a legal document.

DETAIL SHEETS

Becase local codes and requirements vary greatly, we recommend that you obtain drawings and bids from licensed contractors to do your mechanical plans. However, if you want to know more about techniques—and deal more confidently with subcontractors—we offer these remarkably useful detail sheets. Each is an excellent tool that will enhance your understanding of these technical subjects.

Plumbing

The Blueprint Package includes locations for all the plumbing fixtures in your new house, including sinks, lavatories, tubs, showers, toilets, laundry trays and water heaters. However, if you want to know more about the complete plumbing system, these 24x36-inch detail sheets will prove very useful. Prepared to meet requirements of the National Plumbing Code, these six fact-filled sheets give general information on pipe schedules, fittings, sump-pump details, water-softener hookups, septic system details and much more. Color-coded sheets include a glossary of terms.

Electrical

The locations for every electrical switch, plug and outlet are shown in your Blueprint Package. However, these Electrical Details go further to take the mystery out of household electrical systems. Prepared to meet requirements of the National Electrical Code, these comprehensive 24x36-inch drawings come packed with helpful information, including wire sizing, switch-installation schematics, cable-routing details, appliance wattage, door-bell hookups, typical service panel circuitry and much more. Six sheets are bound together and color-coded for easy reference. A glossary of terms is also included.

Construction

The Blueprint Package contains everything an experienced builder needs to construct a particular house. However, it doesn't show all the ways that houses can be built, nor does it explain alternate construction methods. To help you understand how your house will be built—and offer additional techniques—this set of drawings depicts the materials and methods used to build foundations, fireplaces, walls, floors and roofs. Where appropriate, the drawings show acceptable alternatives. These six sheets will answer questions for the advanced do-it-yourselfer or home planner.

Plan-A-Home®

Plan-A-Home® is an easy-to-use tool that helps you design a new home, arrange furniture in a new or existing home, or plan a remodeling project. Each package contains:

- More than *700 peel-off planning symbols* on a self-stick vinyl sheet, including walls, windows, doors, all types of furniture, kitchen components, bath fixtures and many more. All are made of durable, peel-and-stick vinyl you can use over and over.
- A reusable, transparent, *1/4-inch scale planning grid* made of tough mylar that matches the scale of actual working drawings (1/4-inch equals 1 foot). This grid provides the basis for house layouts of up to 140x92 feet.
- *Tracing paper* and a protective sheet for copying or transferring your completed plan.
- A *felt-tip pen*, with water-soluble ink that wipes away quickly.

With Plan-A-Home®, you can make basic planning decisions for a new house or make modifications to an existing house. Use with your Blueprint Package to test modifications to rooms or to plan furniture arrangements before you build. Plan-A-Home® lets you lay out areas as large as a 7,500 square foot, six-bedroom, seven-bath house.

1.

ONE-STORY HOMES
A collection of 470 homes to suit a range of budgets in one-story living. All popular styles, including Cape Cod, Southwestern, Tudor and French. **384 pages. $8.95 ($10.95 Canada)**

2.

TWO-STORY HOMES
478 plans for all budgets in a wealth of styles: Tudors, Saltboxes, Farmhouses, Victorians, Georgians, Contemporaries and more. **416 pages. $8.95 ($10.95 Canada)**

3.

MULTI-LEVEL AND HILL-SIDE HOMES 312 distinctive styles for both flat and sloping sites. Includes exposed lower levels, open staircases, balconies, decks and terraces. **320 pages. $6.95 ($8.95 Canada)**

4.

VACATION AND SECOND HOMES 258 ideal plans for a favorite vacation spot or perfect retirement or starter home. Includes cottages, chalets, and 1-, 1 1/2-, 2-, and multi-levels. **256 pages. $5.95 ($7.50 Canada)**

9.

330 EARLY AMERICAN HOME PLANS A heartwarming collection of the best in Early American architecture. Traces the style from Colonial structures to popular traditional versions. Includes a history of different styles. **304 pages. $9.95 ($11.95 Canada)**

10.

335 CONTEMPORARY HOME PLANS Required reading for anyone interested in the clean-lined elegance of Contemporary design. Features plans of all sizes and types, as well as a history of this style. **304 pages. $9.95 ($11.95 Canada)**

11.

WESTERN HOME PLANS Over 215 home plans from Spanish Mission and Monterey to Northwest Chateau and San Francisco Victorian. Historical notes trace the background and geographical incidence of each style. **208 pages. $8.95 ($10.95 Canada)**

12.

COUNTRY HOUSES Shows off 80 country homes in three eye-catching styles: Cape Cods, Farmhouses and Center-Hall Colonials. Each features an architect's exterior rendering, artist's depiction of a furnished interior room, large floor plans, and planning tips. **208 pages. $10.95 ($12.95 Canada)**

NEW ENCYCLOPEDIA OF HOME DESIGNS
Over 500 plans organized by architectural category including all types and styles and 269 brand-new plans. The most comprehensive plan book ever.

14. 352 pages. $9.95 ($11.95 Canada)

MOST POPULAR HOME DESIGNS
Our customers' favorite plans, including one-story, 1 1/2-story, two-story, and multi-level homes in a variety of styles. Designs feature many of today's most popular amenities: lounges, clutter rooms, media rooms and more.

15. 272 pages. $8.95 ($10.95 Canada)

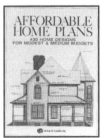

AFFORDABLE HOME PLANS For the prospective home builder with a modest or medium budget. Features 430 one-, 1 1/2- two-story and multi-level homes in a wealth of styles. Included are cost saving ideas for the budget-conscious.

16. 320 pages. $8.95 ($10.95 Canada)

5.

VICTORIAN DREAM HOMES
160 Victorian and farmhouse designs. From Second Empire homes through the Queen Anne and Folk Victorian era. Beautiful renderings accompany the floor plans. **192 pages. $12.95 ($15.95 Canada)**

6.

DECK PLANNER
25 practical plans and details for decks the do-it-yourselfer can actually build. How-to data and project starters for a variety of decks. Construction details available separately. **112 pages. $7.95 ($9.95 Canada)**

7.

THE HOME LANDSCAPER
55 fabulous front- and backyard plans that even the do-it-yourselfer can master. Complete construction blueprints and regionalized plant lists available for each design. **208 pages. $12.95 ($15.95 Canada)**

8.

BACKYARD LANDSCAPER
Contains 40 professionally designed plans for backyards to do yourself or contract out. Complete construction blueprints and regionalized plant lists available. **160 pages. $12.95 ($15.95 Canada)**

13.

COLONIAL HOUSES
161 history-inspired homes with up-to-date plans are featured along with 2-color interior illustrations and 4-color photographs. Included are many plans developed for *Colonial Homes'* History House Series. **208 pages. $10.95 ($12.95 Canada)**

17.

LUXURY DREAM HOMES
A collection of 150 of the best luxury home plans from seven of the most highly regarded designers and architects in the United States. For anyone interested in designing, building or remodeling a luxury home. **192 pages. $14.95 $17.95 Canada)**

Please fill out the coupon below. We will process your order and ship it from our office within 48 hours. Send coupon and check for the total to:

HOME PLANNERS, INC.
3275 West Ina Road, Suite 110, Dept. BK
Tucson, Arizona 85741

THE DESIGN CATEGORY SERIES — A great series of books edited by design type. Complete collection features 1376 pages and 1273 home plans.

1. _____ One-Story Homes @ $8.95 ($10.95 Canada) $ _____
2. _____ Two-Story Homes @ $8.95 ($10.95 Canada) $ _____
3. _____ Multi-Level & Hillside Homes @ $6.95 ($8.95 Canada) $ _____
4. _____ Vacation & Second Homes @ $5.95 ($7.50 Canada) $ _____

NEW FROM HOME PLANNERS

5. _____ Victorian Dream Homes @ $12.95 ($15.95 Canada) $ _____
6. _____ Deck Planner @ $7.95 ($9.95 Canada) $ _____
7. _____ The Home Landscaper @ $12.95 ($15.95 Canada) $ _____
8. _____ Backyard Landscaper @ $12.95 ($15.95 Canada) $ _____

THE EXTERIOR STYLE SERIES

9. _____ 330 Early American Home Plans @ $9.95 ($11.95 Canada) $ _____
10. _____ 335 Contemporary Home Plans @ $9.95 ($11.95 Canada) $ _____
11. _____ Western Home Plans @ $8.95 ($10.95 Canada) $ _____
12. _____ Country Houses @ $10.95 ($12.95 Canada) $ _____
13. _____ Colonial Houses @ $10.95 ($12.95 Canada) $ _____

PLAN PORTFOLIOS

14. _____ New Encyclopedia of Home Designs @ $9.95 ($11.95 Canada) $ _____
15. _____ Most Popular Home Designs @ $8.95 ($10.95 Canada) $ _____
16. _____ Affordable Home Plans @ $8.95 ($10.95 Canada) $ _____
17. _____ Luxury Dream Homes @ $14.95 ($17.95 Canada) $ _____
Sub-Total $ _____
Arizona residents add 5% sales tax; Michigan residents add 4% sales tax $ _____
ADD Postage and Handling $ 3.00
TOTAL (Please enclose check) $ _____

Name (please print) _____

Address _____

City _____ State _____ Zip _____

CANADIAN CUSTOMERS: Order books Toll-Free 1-800-848-2550. Or complete the order form above, and mail with your check indicating U.S. funds to: Home Planners, Inc., 3275 W. Ina Road, Suite 110, Tucson, AZ 85741.

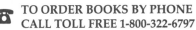 **TO ORDER BOOKS BY PHONE CALL TOLL FREE 1-800-322-6797**

TB21BK

Architectural Antiques Exchange
715 N. Second St.
Philadelphia, PA 19123
(215) 922-3669
FAX (215) 922-3680
doors, entryways, etched glass,
fencing & gates, windows

Anthony Wood Products, Inc.
P.O. Box 1081
Hillsboro, TX 76645
(817) 582-7225
FAX (817) 582-7620
arches, balusters, brackets, corbels,
drops, finials, fretwork,
gable trim, spindles

The Balmer Architectural Art Studios
9 Codeco Ct.
Don Mills, ONT M3A 1B6   Canada
(416) 449-2155
FAX (416) 449-3098
cartouches, centerpieces, festoons,
finials, friezes, keystones, medallions,
mouldings, pilasters, rosettes

Blue Ox Millworks
Foot of X St.
Eureka, CA 95501
(800) 248-4259   (707) 444-3437
FAX (707) 444-0918
balusters, baseboards, door & window
casings, gutters, mouldings, porches,
posts, vergeboards, wainscotting

Cain Architectural Art Glass
Rt. 1 Box AAA
Bremo Bluff, VA 23022
(804) 842-3984
beveled glass, windows, custom
beveling on traditional machinery

Classic Architectural Specialties
3223 Canton St.
Dallas, TX 75226
(214) 748-1668 (in Dallas)
(800) 622-1221
FAX (214) 748-7149
uncommon architectural features

Creative Openings
P.O. Box 4204
Bellingham, WA 98227
(800) 677-6420   (206) 671-6420
screen doors

Cumberland Woodcraft Co.
P.O. Drawer 609
Carlisle, PA 17013
(800) 367-1884 (outside of PA)
(717) 243-0063
FAX (717) 243-6502
balusters, brackets, carvings, corbels,
doors, fretwork, mouldings, screen
doors

Custom Ironwork, Inc.
P.O. Box 180
Union, KY 41091
(606) 384-4122
FAX (606) 384-4848
fencing & gates, furniture

Denninger Cupolas & Weathervanes
RD 1, Box 447
Middletown, NY 10940
(914) 343-2229
cupolas

Elegant Entries
240 Washington St.
Auburn, MA 01501
(800) 343-3432
(508) 832-9898 (in MA)
FAX (508) 832-6874
beveled glass, doors, art glass

Fancy Front Brassiere Co.
P.O. Box 2847
Roseville, CA 95746
(916) 791-7733
FAX (916) 773-2956
balusters, brackets, corbels, gable trim,
posts, screen doors

Focal Point Inc.
P.O. Box 93327
Atlanta, GA 30377-0327
(800) 662-5550   (404) 351-0820
arches, centerpieces, door & window
casings, entryways, festoons, friezes,
keystones, medallions, mouldings,
rosettes

Gothom, Inc.
Box 421, 110 Main St.
Erin, ONT N0B 1T0   Canada
(519) 833-2574   FAX (519) 833-9751
balusters, porches, posts, screen doors,
vergeboards

Hicksville Woodworks Co.
265 Jerusalem Ave.
Hicksville, NY 11801
(516) 938-0171
arches, balusters, fencing & gates,
finials, vergeboards

Mad River Woodworks
Box 1067
Arcata, CA 95525-1067
(707) 668-5671
brackets, drops, entryways, finials,
mouldings, posts, spandrels, wainscotting

W.F. Norman Corporation
P.O. Box 323, 214 N. Cedar
Nevada, MO 64772-0323
(800) 641-4038   (417) 667-5552
FAX (417) 667-2708
balusters, brackets, cartouches, finials,
friezes, keystones, mouldings

The Old Wagon Factory
P.O. Box 1427, Dept. PHE91
Clarksville, VA 23927
(804) 374-5787
screen doors

Ornamental Mouldings Limited
P.O. Box 336
Waterloo, ONT N2J 4A4   Canada
(519) 884-4080
FAX (519) 884-9692
in the United States:
P.O. Box 7123
High Point, NC 27264
baseboards, door & window casings,
mouldings

The Renovators Supply
P100 Renovators Old Mill
Millers Falls, MA 01349
(413) 659-2211   (413) 659-2241
FAX (413) 659-3976
classic hardware, plumbing, lighting and
home decorating items

San Francisco Victoriana, Inc.
2070 Newcomb Ave.
San Francisco, CA 94124
(415) 648-0313
FAX (415) 648-2812
baseboards, brackets, centerpieces, door
& window casings, festoons, medallions,
mouldings, pilasters, posts, rosettes,
wainscotting

Silverton Victorian Millworks
P.O. Box 2987 - HPI
Durango, CO 81302
(800) 933-3930   (303) 259-5915
FAX (303) 259-5919
arches, balusters, baseboards, brackets,
carvings, door and window casings,
drops, keystones, mouldings, pilasters,
porches, posts, screen doors, vergeboards, wainscotting, windows

Tennessee Fabricating Co.
1822 Latham St.
Memphis, TN 38106
(901) 948-3354
brackets, fencing & gates, finials, porches

Vintage Wood Works
Highway 34
Quinlan, TX 75474
(903) 356-2158
arches, balusters, brackets, corbels,
drops, finials, fretwork, gable decora-
tions, porches, posts, spandrels, vergeboards

Wood Factory
901 Harvard
Houston, TX 77008
(713) 863-7600   FAX (713) 863-1183
corbels, doors, gables, mouldings